TRACK RECORD

TRACK RECORD

Me, Music and the War on Blackness

GEORGE THE POET

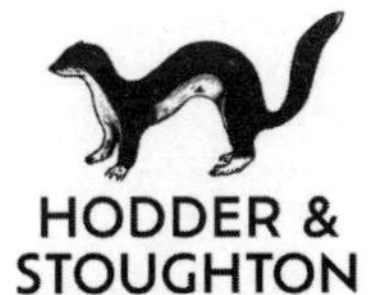

HODDER &
STOUGHTON

First published in Great Britain in 2024 by Hodder & Stoughton Limited
An Hachette UK company

2

Transcribed material from *Have You Heard George's Podcast?*
reproduced in association with George Mpanga

A CIP catalogue record for this title is available from the British Library

Hardback ISBN 9781529341935
ebook ISBN 9781529341942

Typeset in Sabon MT by Hewer Text UK Ltd, Edinburgh
Printed and bound in Great Britain by Clays Ltd, St Ives plc

Hodder & Stoughton policy is to use papers that are natural, renewable and recyclable products and made from wood grown in sustainable forests. The logging and manufacturing processes are expected to conform to the environmental regulations of the country of origin.

Hodder & Stoughton Limited
Carmelite House
50 Victoria Embankment
London EC4Y 0DZ

www.hodder.co.uk

Contents

Part IV: History Rhymes

Dedicated to my wife, Sandra; to our son, Isaiah;
and the ancestors who made us

Introduction

Whenever I'm at a party, I always end up with a small circle of people around me talking passionately. My wife, Sandra, usually looks over and laughs. She knows I can never explain how this keeps happening, and she knows I don't mind. Unless I'm hearing my favourite songs, I'd rather use the occasion to catch up with people or learn about someone new. Luckily, people usually talk to me about things I find interesting, so my listening face isn't forced. To be fair, that's probably why I constantly end up in this position in the first place. One person tells me something genuinely interesting and my listening expression (eyes closed, nodding like I'm in church) makes them share more and more. Someone else takes an interest and jumps in, also sharing from a deep place. Every now and then I throw out another question or suggestion and before you know it, we have a full-blown therapy session in the middle of a party. I found myself in this situation not long ago, but this time it left me pissed off.

I was talking to two women. None of us had met before but one knew who I was and, although the other didn't, she was pursuing a similar academic course to me. Since we were all Black, we ended up talking about Black things. The one who knew of me – let's call her Dee – shared that she worked with kids on a council estate and was concerned that too much of what they heard in the media about their world was negative. The other one – we'll call her Samira – agreed, and said she resented that 'Black' meant 'struggle' in the minds of so many. I identified with their frustration, but barely had a moment to speak before Dee's husband joined the conversation. Let's call him Will.

Like Dee, Will also knew who I was, proudly revealing that he actually introduced his wife to my work, making her a fan ever since. He was full of praise, and I really felt how sincerely he meant every word. This is by far the best part of having a public-facing career – you *connect* with people. But unlike Dee, Will was White, and even more unlike her, he was full of himself. If he's reading this now, I'm sure he'll reject this criticism, but there's no way he left our conversation unaware of how I saw him. Will quickly started preaching to us about how loads of Black people had it all wrong. Apparently, we had bought into the victim narrative that the liberal media imposed on us; in reality, many of us were doing better than a lot of White people. As a father of biracial children, Will didn't want the world teaching his kids about racism because he believed this would only place false limitations on their outlook. As someone who had travelled across Africa ('*No offence guys, but I'm probably more African than you!*'), he had met all sorts of amazing people who didn't see themselves as sufferers of this or that; they were just good, hardworking individuals who earned much less than the Black people complaining about life in this country.

I try not to react strongly to anyone I've just met, but Will made me sick. The whole time he spoke, I silently reminded myself that I didn't have to respond. I could let him say his piece and continue enjoying the party once he – or I – left the conversation. But aside from the fact that this wasn't my nature I was bothered by one thing he said in particular. This guy was actually a father of Brown children who, judging by the adorable pictures he and his wife showed us, would one day be seen as Black people. Didn't this give me a responsibility to offer their dad a different perspective, before it was too late? My disdain for Will's arrogance turned into pity for his wife as the man kept on talking. Neither Samira nor I had said a word, while Dee embarrassedly tried to laugh him off before eventually trying to shut him up. I slowly started to zone out, thinking deeply about what I could say to this guy. If I, of all people, couldn't give him *something* to think about, then what hope was there for his children, who would eventually grow up and struggle to map his logic onto their reality? I imagined these kids leading successful careers full of acceptance speeches at awards shows, in which they thanked their parents, and gave special credit to their father, who always told them that the colour of their skin meant nothing.

As Will continued ejaculating his unsolicited opinions all over our perfectly fine conversation, I tried to cut down the long list of potential responses in my head. Do I point out that Black families own a fraction of the wealth White families own? Or that Black workers tend to earn less than their White counterparts? Nah. He'll find a few examples of privileged Black people and act like that proves something. Ok, what if I link wealth and income inequality to centuries of unpaid labour via slavery and colonialism? Nah. I'm not giving this man a history lesson in this party. Then I realised that was the only point worth making: *this is a party*. Will's rude entry into the conversation came from his lack of awareness – the same lack of awareness that made him overestimate the value of his surface-level opinion. He saw two Black people talking to his Black wife and thought he had something to tell us, without bothering to learn our perspective or earn our respect. It never even occurred to him that we might have been in the middle of saying everything he wanted to say before he joined us. He didn't ask where his wife's new friends stood politically because to him we were just blank slates, waiting to learn from his limited experience. But aside from all this, the biggest problem to address was that his views were dead. Ugly, misinformed crap. By jumping into our conversation with his dead perspective, Will was killing the vibe. So, I told him that.

I started off carefully at first: 'I hear what you're saying bro, but can I be real?' It was a rhetorical question, but he gave me permission anyway. 'When Black people are talking about Black issues, I think you should read the room.' This would be confrontational to a lot of Brits and Ugandans (who both have a culture of passive-aggressive politeness), but, where I grew up, conversations about respect had to be direct. Will shifted his weight uncomfortably and hid his surprise behind a look of curiosity, as he leaned in to hear me better. I continued: 'You didn't ask where we stood on anything, but you kind of explained where Black people are going wrong, from your perspective. You get what I'm saying, bro? And we don't really know each other like that. So, it comes across a bit . . .' I struggled to find a word that wouldn't make things worse '. . . awkward. Just for future reference.'

I don't know what I expected. I said more than intended but less than necessary.

Will shot back immediately. 'Oh, because I'm White?' Even though he tried to keep his tone casual, I could hear the tension in his voice, and it annoyed me.

'Yeah,' I said flatly. My wife would have been more diplomatic, but I had no charm left in me by this point. Dee interjected, sick of the embarrassment.

'Honestly,' she said to Samira and me with a strained smile, 'I tell him this all the time.' Her voice became slightly sharper as she turned to Will: 'Honey, these are sensitive conversations. It wouldn't cost you anything to tread more carefully.' Dee took an exasperated sip from her glass and Will's face turned red as he huffed and scoffed. I felt bad that a marital dispute had come to the surface as a result of what I'd said. Dee was a cool person, and I got the feeling she didn't enjoy publicly siding with a stranger over her husband, but it seemed like a part of her had felt unheard and in need of an ally for a long time.

'Well, I'm sorry,' replied Will, predictably, 'but I don't go for this "because-I'm-White-I'm-not-allowed-an-opinion" thing. You *need* us in this conversation, because without our input nothing will change. Of course, racism is really bad, but you can't fight it with more racism, and by shutting me down because I'm White, that's what you're doing.'

My stomach turned. This guy was the worst kind of stereotype, but he clearly had no clue that, at this moment in 2022, the world had moved on. Yes, it was possible for any White person to live an antiracist life, but not without listening and learning. Will wanted to skip past that stage and teach us to overcome racism with a positive attitude, like many unserious people before him. I never really thought about the term 'White fragility' until I was faced with this grown man struggling to process the fact that he had to earn the right to speak on Black issues, and having an interracial family wasn't enough. How many times had he gaslit his Black wife in this way? My eyes glazed over as I thought about Reni Eddo-Lodge's book, *Why I'm No Longer Talking to White People About Race*.[1] Her whole argument had never resonated with me so deeply.

I became a public figure because I wanted to communicate with people directly. It has taken time for me and many in my life to understand the *dos* and *don'ts* that come with this position, and I've moved with caution. Throughout this journey, informal education has always been my priority, but I've tried not to overstep and talk about things I don't understand. Being a celebrity, it can be easy to forget that the constant interviews and accolades are not an indication that you are genuinely important or even worth listening to; more that the industry platforming you is benefiting in some way from your public presence. This was one of many realisations that hit me throughout my twenties, gradually causing me to listen much more than I spoke. The result was a life of studying my experiences and mapping them onto the world, with the aim of sharing what I learned along the way. I stopped posting all my thoughts on social media and committed to only releasing ones I'd weighed up carefully. *Track Record* is the latest product of that ongoing process: using the thing I know best (my life) to share my own insights about the world.

This book has grown up alongside another one I'm working on: my doctoral thesis (eventually, my PhD). It's a research project I'm doing under the supervision of Economics Professor Mariana Mazzucato at her Institute for Innovation and Public Purpose (IIPP), based at University College London (UCL). The thesis came from my first conversation with Mariana, which was set up by a mutual friend, Tanya Moti. Tanya knew what she was doing when she introduced us. I used to talk her ear off about Black music being a vehicle for community organising, based on the experiences I shared as a young rapper with many across my generation. Tanya realised that Mariana's work on valuable things that are collectively produced would help me develop my ideas. She invited us out for a drink, and it became clear that me and Mariana spoke the same language instantly. I read her books and discovered new ways to explain what I've always seen. But value creation is just one part of music's role in our communities. It's actually a very unfairly rewarded part, but we'll get to that. Another fascinating aspect of music's role in our lives is education – or, more specifically, *pedagogy* – the method of teaching. Again, like many others in my generation I found that Black music unlocked my intellectual capacity, especially when I used it to deal with a problem. This is why my PhD is co-supervised by Dr Karen Edge, a pioneering Professor of Education. Karen booked me for the London Festival of Education back in 2015, when I was still signed to a record deal. The festival helped me see that improving education was my end goal, and Karen wisely pushed me to think about doing a PhD years before I met Mariana. So, my PhD is about the value of Black music, but *Track Record* won't get into all that. I'm doing the doctoral research to get a firm grip on how this music can be used across the Black world for a better future. But *this* book isn't about the future of the Black struggle; it's about the backstory – the track record.

Black people, and the working class in general, live in the space between independence and liberation. We're independent of any real institutional protection and are left to earn our freedom. But we don't do this through collective strategy; we struggle independently, which is why music provides the perfect window into our predicament. It's produced individually but broadcast to the masses, reflecting on us as a group. In truth, though, we're more like a group of individuals than an individual group. And through my journey as a Black artist in the Western world, I've gained a lot of insight into why that is.

First, I'll walk you through my early life, looking at the politics that took me from Rap to Spoken Word. Although our community was full of potential, economic and racial oppression were all around us, so in this section I'll explain how poverty and racism became the core themes of my poetry. Since my community and my secondary school were two different worlds, I ended up learning two worldviews at the same time. The key that unlocked each of them was language, so thoughts on language, community and education feature heavily throughout this book. But you can't separate these thoughts from questions of power, so for this reason we'll track the roots of global inequality all the way back to the European exploitation of Africans and Africa. Another huge realisation of my twenties was how silent Western society had been about the enormous wealth it generated from African flesh, and eventually African land. Despite studying Politics and Sociology in my last years of school and university, nothing I read in all that time explained the central role of human sacrifice and armed robbery in the European rise to power. So, I use this part of *Track Record* to reflect on the confusion caused by that forced forgetfulness. Finally, I describe how a new burst of creativity allowed me to pursue my goal of informally educating. By digging deeper and deeper into my own experiences, I rediscovered the unique opportunity for reflection that music and poetry offer, and used it to release all those thoughts I'd been withholding from social media.

Some days I'm conflicted about writing an autobiographical book, as it feels like there are more important things to talk about than myself. But the truth is that nothing compares to a personal story. I've been through phases of releasing poetry about everything other than my actual life, and I've seen how that has changed the vibe between me and my audience. Of course, I'd be lying if I said the need to make money hasn't also led to compromises. Sometimes my choices haven't matched up to my politics, other times my politics have been undercooked, straight up. But in all, I've worked hard to mould a career that qualifies me to advise young people, and one unavoidable part of that is getting paid, which I've tried my best to do without exploiting anyone. Most Black people in my life don't have the time to reflect on their exploitation, let alone offer economic and political analyses to the next generation. Ironically, that's largely due to their exploitative economic and political circumstances. This injustice stresses me out, but art keeps me sane. Through it, I can convey a world in which Black liberation is at the forefront of Black culture – a fast track into young hearts. This is the most concrete change I can imagine because all other goals unfortunately seem too distant. They usually hinge on the same unlikely condition: that people will one day unite and rise up. As I will explain in this book, our oppressors are the all-time heavyweights of oppression, meaning they've crafted some undefeated ways of preventing that. But Black creativity is also undefeated. That's why I've used my audio-series, *Have You Heard George's Podcast?* (*HYHGP*), to provide some economic and political reflection space using everything I've learned from Black music. Yes, my work is autobiographical, because Black culture has convinced me that all our lives are worth writing about.

We'll return to my conversation with Samira, Dee and Will throughout the following chapters. At the start of Reni Eddo-Lodge's *Why I'm No Longer Talking to White People About Race,* she describes the White obliviousness that has confronted her in countless conversations, which is what Will represented to me that night. In the middle of a party, he reminded me that, as late as 2022, grown adults with kids of their own felt no need to have lived or even *studied* the Black experience before forming and preaching strong opinions on it. The arrogance of this approach is not limited to White people; I've come across loads of Black people who also comment on racial inequality like out-of-shape sports fans coaching professionals through a TV screen. But I relate to their confusion. We haven't inherited a world that treats the Black struggle with respect, so it takes a lot of un-learning to fathom what we're up against. Think I'm exaggerating? Then what's the word for it? Half a millennium of free-to-heavily-discounted labour through chattel slavery, colonisation, debt bondage, over-policed ghettos and institutional racism? This word would have to be the anti-Black version of 'holocaust/mass-rape/mass-torture, multiplied by centuries' all in one. Unsurprisingly, no such word exists in English. In fact, before the killing of George Floyd, many of us in countries like the United Kingdom became used to the word 'Black' being whitewashed out of public life, or buried in the totalising term 'BAME', as if it was insensitive or uncivilised to acknowledge Blackness. But regardless, Blackness has a rich history that we are all part of. As someone who didn't grow up under radical influences, I recognise how hard it can be to connect the present to that history. But by reflecting on our condition using Black cultural works, we can study and document our own track record.

PART I

The Warm-Up

1

The War on Blackness

I want to start by explaining what I mean by the 'War on Blackness'. It's not a phrase I heard growing up and still doesn't feature heavily in mainstream English, but evidence of it is all around us. *Track Record* is not an encyclopaedia of the war; it's more like the story of how I came to terms with it. For this reason, I encourage my readers to look beyond this book for a fuller understanding of how the war works. In the following pages, I will describe aspects of it that have played out in my life, and how a lack of real political education leads many like me to fight for the wrong side. But first we need to define the conflict, so, what is the War on Blackness?

'Blackness' refers to the lived experience and political context of people racialised as Black. This includes the aspects of our lives that we haven't necessarily signed up for, like being seen as 'Black' in the first place. A lot of people reject the term and I understand why. It's a Eurocentric reduction, a totalisation of who we are that has been used to flatten our beauty, range and nuance. I feel all of that, but I also feel that our struggle and our connection to Africa binds us together in a racial experience. And I take pride in this, so I embrace the classification of Blackness.

The War on Blackness is an umbrella term for the long-running assault on Black life perpetrated by the former colonial powers of Europe and their offshoots, which we will refer to as *the West*. In this book, I speak passionately about the track record of injustice that has been inflicted on Black people by the West, but this is not an indictment of every White person who ever lived. In referring to the West, I'm usually talking about the ruling classes of Western Europe and their settler colonies, such as North America and Australasia. This group of people have, for hundreds of years, exerted a disproportionate, divisive and violent influence on the rest of the world. The working classes of their own countries are more heavily exploited today than they were fifty years ago, currently struggling to find democratic representation in a political climate hostile to working people. For this reason, I try not to assume that the actions of the Western ruling class completely reflect the attitudes of the Western working class. However, the West has secured such a wide gap between the material conditions it enjoys and those experienced across the rest of the planet, that even the masses of Westerners who would like a more equal world cannot avoid the advantages of this inequality.

These advantages also extend to those of us in the Black diaspora, although our lives out here are shaped by the racial hierarchy, too. It feels awkward to admit this, especially as someone who has focused their career on diaspora issues, but proximity to White power can have a disorienting effect on Black people. Energy we would have given to the challenges of our homelands is instead diverted to addressing the much narrower experience of being an ethnic minority in the West. Often, we spend more time fighting for a bigger share of our colonisers' looted wealth than we do ending the West's continued exploitation of our ancestral homes. This dilemma is embodied in the Foundational Black American (FBA) movement of the United States, which sees the interests of people descended from enslaved Africans in America as separate from (and often competing with) the interests of other Black groups – including those enslaved and terrorised elsewhere. The FBA movement's tunnel-visioned focus on reparations for Black Americans alone is indicative of the division created by proximity to White power; in this case, the power to share out wealth deriving from genocide, slavery and exploitation.

The Colonial Skeleton

We all live in a racial hierarchy rooted in colonialism. Colonialism was a stretch of history when violence and scarcity across Europe forced Europeans to find development prospects beyond the continent. Once they located these prospects in other lands, Western powers did one or more of the following: they established increasingly unbalanced trade relationships with the richer regions, which they violently excluded their European neighbours from; where they had the upper hand militarily, they cleared the land through genocide in order to establish their own societies, enslaving whatever natives were left; and, of course, they built enormous economic power using an unpaid workforce of enslaved Africans. Over the centuries, these models of colonialism were adapted to appear more humane, but their outcomes stayed the same: resource extraction and racial hierarchy. A lot of people struggle to wrap their heads around this reality because the racial hierarchy is not obvious to them. Poor White communities and high-flying Black professionals are taken as proof that racism isn't as real as it used to be. This view is only possible if you focus on individual examples and ignore the global differences in wealth between races. Once you start looking into it, it doesn't take long to learn that the West has a lot more than everyone else. This colonial basis of Western wealth led sociologist Cedric

Robinson to coin the phrase *racial capitalism*, describing the racist DNA of what has become our global economic system.[2] Understanding this concept is like having economic X-ray vision: it helps you see the colonial skeleton underneath capitalism's outward appearance.

For example, the brown sugar in our supermarkets is labelled 'Demerara', after the plantation colony of British Guiana (now Guyana) that supplied the minimally refined product to Western markets. The sugar industry is full of colonial skeletons. August 2023 marked the two hundredth anniversary of a slave rebellion in Demerara, in which over ten thousand enslaved Africans staged a non-violent uprising against their White oppressors, contributing significantly to Britain's abolition of slavery ten years later. Tragically, the resistance was defeated, and its leaders were put to death by the British. Yet Britain did nothing to honour the bicentennial of this horrific episode, despite defenders of empire proudly pointing to abolition as evidence of the country's moral leadership. In fact, when Guyanese-descended Member of the British Parliament David Lammy asked in 2022 if the UK government would grant pardons to those imprisoned and executed over the rebellion, then-Justice Secretary Dominic Raab brushed the request aside, replying that since Guyana is now independent, those pardons would be the responsibility of the Guyanese president. But let's look beyond this shameful example of colonial denialism, towards the system's important economic legacy.

Post-abolition, ownership of Demerara's sugar production remained in the hands of English capitalists, who – as well as receiving government compensation for the loss of slave income – imported a class of indentured workers from India to continue production, instead of just paying the formerly enslaved Africans. This ownership dynamic, plus the movement of whole demographics across the world in service of Western industry, gives us a clear snapshot of racial capitalism. Deniers of racism want to downplay the extent to which Guyana's colonial skeletons reflect the overall anatomy of world trade, but in reality, this tale of exploitation is worldwide. By the time of Guyana's independence in the 1960s, Demerara's sugar industry was still owned by Western capitalists, with the former colonial master Booker-McConnell controlling 85 per cent of sugar production, which translated to one third of the economy, 13 per cent of the workforce and 40 per cent of Guyana's foreign-exchange income. In true imperial style, Booker-McConnell spent the twentieth century whitewashing its reputation through a few schemes to marginally improve the lives of its poor workers, and famously launched the Booker Prize for Fiction, initially awarded to writers from the so-called Commonwealth. Regardless, the living conditions of those descended from the enslaved and indentured workers of Demerara offer further insight into the workings of racial capitalism. After independence, Guyana ended up as one of the poorest countries in the world with one of the highest suicide rates (double the global average). Mass migration became the norm, while the country's politics was plagued with racial tension between the Indo- and Afro-Guyanese populations, which was stoked by Western capital to secure continued access to cheap labour and natural resources. Meanwhile, like a lot of colonial-era companies, Booker-McConnell branched off into other industries, obscuring the root of its wealth in the process.

A War That's Visible Yet Invisible

When you point out the highly visible dynamics of racial capital, a lot of Westerners get defensive – including many Black and Brown people. I guess it comes from not wanting to feel complicit in something unfair. It's uncomfortable being confronted with the injustice of a situation you've accepted or benefited from and, for many, the urge to push back without any real data is too tempting to resist. Later in this book, I'll walk you through a time in my life when I was like this. I felt confident in my own ability to find success in Britain, and that self-confidence grew into overconfidence in the system. Without studying the reality beyond my own life, I drew conclusions about how the world works based on what I saw around me. This is a common mistake that our education system indirectly fosters by not making social and economic analysis compulsory learning. Each of our lives is a drop in the ocean of human experience, and the waters around us can't teach us about currents elsewhere. There really is no substitute for studying the world. Very few can do it casually and develop a serious analysis.

When it comes to understanding Black life in particular, it's easy to get your facts twisted. Propaganda is media intended to influence us politically, and to some extent, all media does this. In the same way that the flavours of a good cocktail hide the taste of alcohol, effective propaganda often dresses up political messages in entertainment. Examples include the positive portrayal of the CIA in Ryan Coogler's 2018 movie *Black Panther*, and the over-focus on Malcolm X's criminal past in Spike Lee's 1992 biopic, X. By framing a CIA agent as a friend of the fictional African country Wakanda, *Black Panther* hides the agency's murderous role in the theft of Africa's wealth. And by spending too much time on less important aspects of Malcolm's life, *X* leaves no room for his super-important international politics. Given the visibility of such misleading propaganda in highly influential Western media, it's complacent to pass judgement on Black issues without unplugging from the mainstream and studying how history played out. The War on Blackness feeds on that complacency. Developing countries' debts can be dismissed as cultural issues of indiscipline and corruption, because underreported Western sabotage has made us think that darker populations are less hardworking. Irregular migration can be framed as the illegal intrusion of freeloaders who want to crash the party, because racist Western news media normalise this view. The racial hierarchy of the workplace can be disconnected from its colonial roots because the so-called liberal democratic societies of the West insist that darker people now have a level playing field. Somehow the War on Blackness is both visible and invisible.

The story of Demerara illustrates a lot about the War on Blackness. Firstly, it shows that the war is deeply rooted in the Western desire to control land, labour and commodities. Secondly, with the inclusion of indentured workers from India, it shows the war as one part of a wider assault on all non-White peoples at the hands of Western capital. However, this is one of those things that is invisible to many in the West, despite the mountains of evidence on display every day. Like the merciless loan-repayment demands imposed on global South nations by Western financial institutions – many of which created these countries' debts in the first place. Or the difference in treatment between Ukrainian refugees and those from the Arab and African world. In London, the racial hierarchy is visible in the staffing of most corporate buildings. You walk through these massive doors into a slickly designed reception area in which the security, cleaners and receptionists are Black and Brown, while everyone else proceeding upstairs to do business is White.

What's the Point of the War on Blackness?

The many interlocking agendas of this war can be summarised in one: maintaining an unbalanced order.

Through the lens of racial capitalism we can see that the colonial empires of Europe created flows of value out of the colonies back to the metropole (the master country). Yes, colonisers built infrastructure here and there, sometimes even providing a little education, but it was *always* for the purpose of extracting something. Colonial railways went from the mines or the fields straight to the port for shipping. Colonial schools only taught enough to train obedient workers. Britain was the most successful at this, with wealth pouring in from Jamaica to India. Being forced to give up these empires after World War Two turned Western Europe into an abusive ex, denying they were ever invested while insisting the abuse was consensual. For this reason, most Western powers haven't even apologised for their enslavement of Africans and genocide of indigenous people, let alone paid reparations. Meanwhile, their right-wing media protest loudly against being made to feel uncomfortable about this history. The problem is, of course, all that denial keeps history alive. Western dominance is upheld by crimes rooted in the past, meaning the world order would be called into question if the West was held truly accountable, which is why there is a permanent War on Blackness.

Sabotage

The assassination of Black leaders by Western powers is a key component of this war. Such killings have usually targeted one person in order to throw off a whole movement. With many of these executions having been led by Western intelligence agencies and carried out by Black perpetrators, we may never get the full scope of political assassinations across Black history, but a few high-profile examples give us some insight. Patrice Lumumba, the Democratic Republic of Congo's first elected leader, is one of the best-known cases. His 1961 murder came early on in the African independence movement and has long since been confirmed as a collaborative project between the CIA, the Belgian government and British intelligence. The 1987 assassination of Burkina Faso's revolutionary leader Thomas Sankara is discussed much less in the English-speaking West than that of Lumumba – probably because it's more recent. Similarly, though, extensive US and French involvement has since been uncovered. This strategy is nothing new; in many ways, America's whole history is based on the killing of African leaders, with the Transatlantic Slave Trade relying on cycles of conflict between African polities. In recent history, the FBI has been implicated in the murders of Malcolm X, Martin Luther King, Fred Hampton, Huey Newton and Tupac Shakur, to name a few. Although the state propaganda machine has been good at framing discussion of government agencies' links to these assassinations as 'conspiracy' theories, what the mainstream media offer instead is a bunch of *coincidence* theories, or plain silence. Regardless, the execution of Black leaders has proven useful and politically inexpensive for the West. It instils fear, knocks morale, kills momentum and often breeds division, especially when the executioners themselves are Black. Furthermore, this use of Black executioners conveniently feeds into the idea that Black people can't govern themselves, reinforcing tropes of excessive violence and selfishness, which all sounds so familiar to propagandised ears that many never bother to question the patterns behind these killings. But the outcome is consistent: by exterminating influential thinkers and political organisers, the West has been able to sidestep democracy and the rule of law for the purpose of maintaining dominance over Black life.

Art and the War on Blackness

In writing this book, I've had to ask myself what the point is in saying any of this. I could have given you a self-promotional story about my life and used it to generate business within the same system I'm criticising. Plus, if the West is so powerful, aren't I wasting my time by critiquing it, knowing that we can't escape this abusive relationship? The thing is, when I had no real opinions on capitalism, I didn't mind self-promotion. I was never good at it, but I wouldn't have had a problem using this book only to tell you about things I've overcome. There are actually people in my family who would rather I did more of that than what I'm doing now. But studying the War on Blackness has helped me to realise that as a Black artist, I'm politically useful to a system that promotes individualised success. Anything I say can be separated from its Third World context and used by the White media to undermine my people's struggle, as the following chapter will demonstrate. But the Black radicals of history have taught us all the importance of speaking up. Critique is the first step towards reimagining our world without the economic cannibalism of today. By keeping quiet, I would be accepting defeat in the War on Blackness because the ultimate goal of this war is *obedience*.

To maintain order, the Western ruling class needs the workers of the world to cooperate in their own exploitation. Without this cooperation, the ruling class has to impose its will through the use of force, like sending the police to violently break up protests. But when that force is applied too loosely, people are more willing to stand up to their oppressors, as could be seen in the protests across France throughout 2023. This scenario is generally avoided through an unwritten contract between rich and poor, whereby the wealthy offer bribes and distractions that keep the masses passive enough to continue being exploited. These tactics include splitting the working class into tiers of privilege – so that workers with slightly higher income and/or status than others are discouraged from struggling against the system – or force-feeding the masses an unhealthy but highly addictive media diet. The War on Blackness entails this and much more, all for the purpose of neutralising Black politics. Why? Because Black people have more reason than most to resent capitalism, which is what makes their complicity so valuable. Across my own lifespan, I've watched radical Black music become co-opted by the rich to focus less on the struggle and more on the pursuit of wealth and, eventually (as epitomised by Jay-Z), reframing the struggle *as* the pursuit of wealth. Is it a coincidence that this change has catapulted Hip Hop to the status of a bestselling music genre worldwide? Of course not. As I will explore throughout this book, the role of music in the War on Blackness is extensive. It can be used to capture hearts and minds, especially of young people, and to misdirect Black politics.

From a young age, I've had an on-and-off relationship with Rap music that struggled under the weight of these contradictions. I loved the sound and the skill of Rap, but couldn't shake the suspicion that it was distorting my perception of Blackness. By the time I was old enough to control my music consumption, Rap had lost the variety it started with through its journey from low-income Black communities to the mainstream. At the turn of the century, it reached young listeners like me via anthems of selfishness and self-destruction, laced with generational trauma. Bizarrely, Black people who opposed mainstream Rap on ethical and political grounds were made to look out of touch. It is only through learning about the many complex, secretive operations run by Western powers to destabilise Black life that I can now make sense of what happened to Hip Hop. As the American academic and political activist Dr Jared A. Ball said, 'White supremacist capital understands . . . you can't sell [capitalism] to White audiences better than through the use of Black cultural expression.' Hip Hop was a culture that, among other things, turned performance into money. The profit-driven music industry ignored those other things and followed the money, investing in performance, but not culture. So Hip Hop, the youth movement, became mainstream Rap, the free-for-all. It's therefore no surprise that the genre now celebrates authenticity in wealth and anti-Black violence above all. Rappers are celebrated for having money and/or for being in conflict with others like them. Think about that: of all the death attached to this music, there's no mainstream rapper whose popularity stems from anti-imperialist violence. Like any other political assassination, this was not a democratic outcome; just another covert operation in the War on Blackness.

Adding to the confusion is the fact that Rap appears to represent Black people. Our music taste is shaped by what's available to us, and as generations of Black children grow up under the influence of mainstream music, many of us subconsciously subscribe to the image of Blackness promoted in Rap.

People say exploitation is just human nature, and that the West's brutal ascent has been attempted by all societies in some way, shape or form. But I can only hear this as propaganda. Mainstream media and education are full of these little myths that try to project Western psychology onto everyone else, as if all of humanity can be explained through the actions of a few Europeans. In reality, it can never be proven that every society has desired or tried to dominate the world and, anyway, the majority of recorded human history doesn't support this notion. Still, even if there is truth to the idea, Western terrorism isn't just a historical fact; it remains the defining feature of our geopolitical landscape. This is why we must study the War on Blackness and learn to recognise its battlefronts in our lives and careers. We have a responsibility to fight, and to win.

2

Stay Woke

A Lecture, an Article and a Tweet

In my thirteen-year career, I'm happy to say I've only been dragged on Twitter (now X) once. For those who don't know, being 'dragged on Twitter' in the 2020s means having a lot of people talking about you negatively on one of the world's most popular social media platforms. Luckily for me it wasn't that serious, but I did learn a lot from the experience. It all started in November 2021, when the *Guardian* published an article based on an interview I gave them. This interview was about an upcoming lecture I would be delivering on prison education for the Longford Trust, a charity that offers scholarships to ex-offenders. Every year the charity invites someone prominent to speak on the importance of educational opportunity for those caught up in the criminal-justice system and based on work I had been doing in prisons for years, in 2021 they reached out to me. I happily accepted their invitation to speak and agreed to do this interview as part of their PR strategy ahead of the lecture. A *Guardian* journalist named Vanessa Thorpe called me and asked about the poetry workshops I'd run with National Prison Radio, as well as my thoughts on prison education in general. The conversation went well, and I looked forward to the article's publication, but when it came my heart sank. I felt that the title was a mess: *George the Poet: 'It's easier to change the lives of offenders in prison than it is on the outside.'* To me, this sounded like I was saying 'lock people up – it's the only way to help them', which I wasn't. What I did say was that prison time could be constructive, as long as prisoners were given the right support. I talked about the need for government to invest in rehabilitation, and the importance of not just wanting better, but *expecting* better lives for prison-leavers. Looking back now, I realise this was a lose-lose game. In Vanessa's defence, I think she represented my views fairly throughout the article, but the racist and classist nature of Britain's criminal-justice system was the real issue that I hadn't addressed, and the title of the article didn't help. If you saw my face next to a quote saying, 'It's easier to change the lives of offenders in prison than it is on the outside,' you could think my profile as a young Black Cambridge-educated poet from a low-income area was being used to make a crooked system seem fair, and I couldn't argue with that. But it gets worse.

Within hours the article started drawing the attention of Twitter users who were, understandably, not impressed. Now, if you know anything about Twitter, you know that people don't always separate criticism from straight disrespect. One guy in particular took it far, depicting me as a 'parasite leeching off the trauma and damage of those incarcerated to feed his own "creativity"' before claiming he wanted to fight me and vomit in my face. Can't lie, he got my attention. I checked his profile and saw that he had a few thousand followers, which kind of bothered me – what if his misrepresentation of my views spread to all those people? Against my better judgement, I replied a few times, defending myself but not reciprocating his disrespect. Again, this was a lose-lose game; nothing I said would change this guy's view, and, like all keyboard warriors, the low likelihood that we would ever meet removed the normal rules of dialogue from his mind. But my attention shifted away from him, as more and more people spoke out against the article, some generally insulting me, others more specific in their critique. In my heated state, I started to see them all as one. This is an easy trap for public figures to fall into: thinking you can absorb hundreds, sometimes thousands of opinions and respond like it's a normal conversation. It's not. The different arguments, respect levels and positionality of each commentator can make it impossible for you to address, or even understand everything at once. Sometimes your only option is to shut up, which my wife, Sandra, advised me to do. Like many regretful husbands before me, I made the mistake of ignoring her advice. I replied to one woman who criticised the article for framing prison as a fairy-tale experience, and this time I was less restrained. I can't find the tweet now because I deleted it, but I said something along the lines of, 'People are locked up. They need support. I'm addressing that through my work. What do you do to address the issues you're passionate about?' Reflecting on that tweet, all I can now think is 'lose-lose-lose'. How the hell did I expect that to go? Fair enough, I felt misjudged, and fair enough, my tweet wasn't crazy, but by my normal standards I was getting lost in the sauce. After years of watching celebrity witch-hunts on social media, I was reacting badly to the fact it was my turn. All those tweets claiming I wanted more prisons to be built, and that I exploited my community for fame then betrayed them once I'd made it – they warped my view. I saw these people as reactionary, attention-seeking performers who didn't bother to do their research before dragging my name through the mud. I was sure that if they checked my track record, they'd see that it was crazy to portray me as an exploiter and traitor of the working class. I couldn't fit this all into a tweet though, so I said something along the lines of, 'This is the problem with woke culture.

Instead of . . .' blah blah blah. I can't even remember the rest of it because, again, I deleted the tweet later. Little did I know at the time, all hell was about to break loose.

As a public figure, the minute your words leave your mind and enter the mind of the public they stop being yours alone – they now belong to everyone. This means that the intent behind those words is no longer the only thing defining their impact. Anyone in a relationship knows the stress of this dilemma. When your words reach someone else's ears, that person might hear something you didn't mean, and even though you may want to 'correct' them, they're not necessarily wrong. People are free to interpret your words however they want, as much as you're free to say whatever you want. So how do you make yourself understood in this minefield of misunderstanding? In my experience, the key is knowing when to push back, and when to let go. On social media, everyone's words are open to interpretation, and everyone has to set their own policy on pushing back and letting go, depending on what's important to them. When I included the phrase 'woke culture' in my tweet, I wasn't looking for a fight. In that moment of frustration, I was pushing back against what I felt were lazy, uninformed performances of political awareness. And this is how public figures trap themselves in public arguments. Yes, some people were speaking from a lazy and uninformed place by describing me as an advocate for prison expansion, but a lot of the criticism coming my way was actually about the framing of prisons in the article. The woman I replied to wasn't wrong for disliking the right-wing slant of the whole piece. I actually shared that dislike, which I explained to her once we got a dialogue going. She clarified that she wasn't attacking me personally, and I clarified that I had overreacted to her because of the rush of bad vibes I was receiving. She and I ended our exchange respectfully, and I'm grateful to that sister for taking the time to educate me. But the next day, things got worse.

I hadn't yet deleted my tweets, since I didn't see anything wrong with them. After that back-and-forth, I'd spent the rest of the day playing games with my nephews and by the following morning, I had actually forgotten about the whole thing . . . until a certain someone got hold of my 'woke culture' tweet. This person had the biggest following of anyone who'd responded so far, and it showed in the level of engagement that her commentary triggered. I can't find it now, but she quote-tweeted a response to me along the lines of, 'What do you mean by "woke culture"? Celebrities don't have the range to engage with criticism, so they throw around the word "woke" to dismiss people fighting for justice.' This tweet got hundreds of interactions in minutes, causing me to respond. I pointed out that I *did* engage with the criticism offered by the woman from my original tweet, and we had reached a mutual understanding. This new commentator shot back that I owed this woman an apology that was as loud as my apparent disrespect. Honestly, I can't remember much after that because, from the cascade of angry tweets that flooded my mentions accusing me of misogynoir – a term coined by Black feminist writer Moya Bailey meaning misogyny against Black women (both tweeters were Black) – I got the message.

'Woke' had become one of those words heavily associated with a certain attitude: specifically, White, right-wing hostility to progressive politics. This shift was epitomised in March of 2023, when British TV presenter Jeremy Vine dismissed the original definition of 'woke' given by social-justice campaigner Natasha Devon on his own show, preferring the more recent corruption of the word. This incident was a textbook example of how language is used as a political tool – a recurring theme in this book. Here, a privileged middle-aged man laughed and condescended his way through a conversation with a younger, better-informed woman in order to dictate the terms of a political debate. Vine said, '"Woke" is basically when you sort of . . . read the *Guardian* and this and that . . .', invoking a burst of laughter from someone else in the studio. Devon replied that '"Woke" is actually an African American term; it means to be awake to injustice in society,' to which Vine replied, 'In *your* definition it means that, but not to everyone,' ignoring the fact that Devon's was the dictionary definition. A clip of this interaction was posted to the TV show's Twitter account, but deleted once it was exposed for its ridiculousness. To me, it perfectly captured the life cycle of the word 'woke' in British culture.

Reflecting on my own Twitter drama, I now can't believe I had carelessly used the word in this way: to hit back against people that I saw as fake-deep, which (as many pointed out to me) was a gaslighting technique honed by right-wing Western media. I should have known better. I'd seen White media figures using 'woke' dismissively for years – they even used it against me – but I was used to Black people also using it as shorthand for performative awareness. In my 'woke culture' tweet, I assumed I could choose how the word would be interpreted when *I* said it. But the thing is, 'woke' wasn't used negatively until it entered the White mainstream. White commentators, who didn't relate to the hard lessons that shaped the politics behind the word, used it sarcastically and patronisingly. So, with my tweet, I was basically invoking a White conservative corruption of a Black radical word against a valid critique made by a Black woman. To this day, the thought of it makes me cringe. If I understood this context better, I still might have made the point about social media reactionaries, but I would never have linked it to 'woke culture'. In this respect, I was out of touch.

The fallout from my little Twitter moment in many ways reflects the changes this book has been through. When I think about the lead up to that situation, I see that I hadn't been paying enough attention to how other people felt; specifically, people who I considered allies in the same struggle I was committed to. If I had been paying more attention, I would have known that taking up mainstream media space to discuss the carceral system without highlighting its racist and classist nature was a bad move. If I had been paying more attention, I would have realised that an interview about prisons for a centrist newspaper like the *Guardian* wouldn't necessarily give me space to present a radical critique of the system, unless I made it my business to do so. If I had been paying more attention, I would have acknowledged the tension between my position as a 'good' immigrant from a two-parent home, who completed school without ever seeing the inside of a cell, and the prison population, in which traumatic childhood experiences and school exclusions were hugely over-represented. Furthermore, I would have realised that my track record of social-justice work didn't automatically excuse me from criticism. Ten years of fame can cause you to forget these things, but I guess we all hide our egos behind good intentions from time to time.

It's possible that no one else has thought about my Twitter incident since then but, even still, I'd like to take this time to apologise for misusing the word 'woke' like that. I'd also like to thank those who tweeted me with the aim of explaining why my language was problematic – you guys genuinely helped me grow. Now, think back to Will, from the party in the Introduction. As a White man, he saw me and Samira, a Black woman, talking to his wife, Dee, who was also Black, and proceeded to tell us all that Black people were more privileged than we realised. I'd like to think my controversial tweets weren't as off-base as his comments, but I do see similarities between our respective mistakes. You can't make sense of society through your experiences alone. That's why this book started off as an inward look at lessons from my life, but as it progressed, its scope expanded. As well as re-telling my own story, I started writing about the world in general, past and present. This has helped me to avoid the mistake I made on Twitter, by situating my perspective within a much bigger picture. So don't be thrown off if I change direction every now and then. Sometimes I'll focus sharply on one aspect of my life, other times I'll step back and look at a big chunk of history; doing both can help us all understand each other better.

One of the best outcomes of the Twitter episode was a much sharper Longford lecture than what I originally wrote. Instead of trying to make people smile with nice stories about prison-leavers who turned their lives around, I delivered a more urgent message: the game is rigged.

> Fifty-four per cent of young people in prison have been in care, compared with less than 1 per cent of all children. Fifty-two per cent of children in custody are from a minority ethnic background . . . The game is rigged. And everyone in this room knows it.

Instead of leaving this unsaid, or assuming that the people in the audience would catch the message elsewhere, I used my Longford lecture to directly address the classist, racist character of the carceral system. Eventually, I made the point that prison education should nurture consciousness among our brothers and sisters behind bars. It's a simple idea but it's so far from reality that I feel naive even saying it out loud.

> Our ability to transform prisons from punishment centres that fail to stop the majority of first-time releases from reoffending into development centres that help people understand and combat the forces pulling them into self-destruction – that's a question of vision.

Looking back, I can see how much I've changed since then. Even though the speech went well, I'm not writing anything like it again – *anything* that endorses any element of the criminal-justice system – because I don't believe we can dismantle the master's house using the master's tools. If you expect prisons to end the cycle of imprisonment that torments the same communities over and over, then you must believe that the game *isn't* rigged. If you think you can trick the system into freeing the oppressed, by feeding into its incentive structures, like making money or providing a 'cost-effective' solution to a widespread problem, then you're not reading the room. The fact is, until poor people and marginalised minorities somehow gain the political power to govern themselves, they will always be trapped in rich people's plans. When I delivered my Longford lecture, I hadn't fully come to terms with this. Regardless, speaking publicly on structural reform through that lecture was a privilege, and I'm grateful to the Longford Trust for that. I'm also grateful to Eva and the Key4Life team, Reem and Marcelline at HMP/YOI Feltham, Natalie, Muna and the team at National Prison Radio, who gave me space to reason with people inside, and reach over eighty thousand others on tour behind the door.

Still, fighting injustice *for real* means using your time to organise solutions. It's hard to do that while also working within the system: *work isn't neutral*. Every minute you spend cultivating one plant is a minute lost cultivating another, and no two plants are the same. For this reason, I'm most grateful to the community that planted seeds of understanding in my mind early on, and showered them with experiences. Being a lot poorer and Blacker than most of the country, this community gave me an alternative view from the mainstream's, and by moving in and out of it (first through school, then later through my career), I've lived in the gaps and the overlaps between different walks of life.

Black Liberals and Black Radicals

St Raphael's Estate, the closed-off North West London neighbourhood I grew up in, stands between the world-famous Wembley Stadium and the global megastore IKEA. Back in the 2000s, these huge businesses employed a few of us, but that employment was rarely life-changing. They usually paid enough to keep us dependent, and recruited locally at junior levels. However, a much bigger employer than both of them was the streets. People refused to accept the economic exclusion set out for them, and risked their freedom for a chance to expand their options. Grappling with this thought process since my teens opened my eyes to the true nature of our problems. My formal education didn't really engage with this reality, but that weird silence was actually a massive hint that something was off. Over the years, as I slowly realised that the power of the streets was economic, I came to understand that unemployment and incarceration were as much a part of the economy as anything else – i.e. Britain has never had a plan to end either of them. There are two ways of handling this depressing reality. In his

2010 doctoral thesis *Back to Black* (later published as a book), pioneering Professor of Black Studies Kehinde Andrews lays out the first approach – the liberal approach – like this:

> Black liberals view [racial disadvantage] as a problem of . . . society not allowing fair access to the Black population. . . . For the Black liberal then, the solution lies in gaining better access to mainstream society.[3]

This liberal approach had me spending a lot of my twenties supporting prisoners and prison leavers within the system. Long term, my vague aim was to intervene in the lives of marginalised young people through an educational service. This service would use my personal template of critical art to create reflection space and entrepreneurial opportunities for street people, utilising their own experiences as course material. It was a liberal strategy. This plan didn't challenge the status quo too much and allowed me to work within the system to increase the access of young Black people to the mainstream job market. Some days this sounds like a long shot, others it seems like a plan that could work, given the right circumstances. But honestly, there was another reason I spent so much time working in prisons.

When I was younger, as I mentioned, my community provided non-mainstream perspectives that made me question the way things were. Later, as an adult who no longer spent as much time in the neighbourhood, I felt the need to actively maintain a connection to it: specifically, the street element. Throughout the first half of this book, I'll explain how that connection developed in the first place, but for now it's enough to say that the streets have always given me the news that doesn't make it to TV. By dialoguing with people who live in the shadows of society, you see what gets hidden from the mainstream, and that awareness strengthens your grip on reality. This kind of dialogue, which flows so naturally in the streets, is closely linked to the second approach that Kehinde Andrews outlined: the radical approach.

> A Black radical approach . . . argues that far from being the solution, the mainstream is in fact the problem . . . it works to oppress the Black population. From this position Black people need to come together as Black people in a wider Diaspora, to create our own futures (Garvey, 1967/1923).

Basically, instead of trying to change the rules of a rigged game, Black radicalism isn't playing. In the mind of a Black radical, no amount of representation will end racism, and to water the garden of diversity is to neglect the real grassroots struggle. So, what does this mean for my work in prisons? Honestly, to create an educative, entrepreneurial space for prisoners through art is better than nothing, but in the face of structural oppression, it's not much. Firstly, this plan needs money, and that money is likely to come from liberal society – businesses and individuals who are financially secure enough to help out. Once upon a time it would have been the government's job to fund social change, but right now governments are stingier than ever, meaning the taxes we pay rarely go towards improving the lives of marginalised people. Secondly, the plan requires the consent and participation of prisons, which creates a conflict of interest, given that so many of them are now privately run businesses. What business wants to admit that it's not fixing the problem it exists for? The point is my prison plan was liberal, not radical. Radical would be spending my life organising a permanent pivot away from the streets and the mainstream job market across as many Black communities as possible. The word 'radical' comes from the Latin 'radix', meaning 'root'. A radical solution gets to the root of a problem.

Privilege

Still, as much as I want radical change to end poverty and injustice, I'm rooted in Western liberal society. And I'll be honest, this makes it hard to avoid participating in things that hurt people. For example, this whole book was written on electronic devices made available to me by slave labour in the Congo – laptops and phones that rely on minerals ripped out of African soil, causing mass destruction of life not far from the land of my ancestors. My career benefits from the same media industry that maintains silence on real, human-made disasters, like the erasure of Palestine. This media happily platforms me as a non-threatening Black man, but also monetises the trauma of my people in ways that uphold White supremacy, while muffling the voices and warping the images of disobedient Black, Brown and even White people – like Julian Assange. I want radical change, but I'm still learning. In fact, it's more accurate to say I'm unlearning. Letting go of the assumption that things are getting better is the first step towards ending so many ongoing atrocities. We have to unlearn the boxes we are put in, so that we can think outside of them; but, as long as our schools and careers keep us busy maintaining the status quo, we'll never find radical solutions to our problems. For this reason, I've kept a low profile throughout most of my career, scarred by the times I've collaborated with someone, or worked with an organisation or endorsed a message that turned out to be weird. But I'm not just hiding from the world, as I hope this book will make clear. I've been *in community* with the people.

Being among the masses and not allowing fame to isolate you is like fighting a losing battle for most celebrities. On the extreme end, your superstardom can weave a cocoon of privilege around you, and if you live in this cocoon for too long the thought of leaving it, or having it breached, becomes very scary. But to me, the real danger is disconnection from everyone else. And for the rare celebrity who prioritises solidarity with the working class over personal privilege, this disconnection can throw your whole life off track. Your understanding of how people feel is filtered through whoever you get your information from, and because you're not out there yourself, you become dependent on those sources of information, none of which are fully neutral. For celebrities who don't value living in community with working people, this isolation is a prize, not a problem. The whole game they are playing is about being *better*, having *more*, feeling *desired*, so they proudly define themselves by the barriers separating them from the masses. The Business Class sections of the airport; the extra layer of protection from private security firms; the tax avoidance schemes unavailable to most. These are all part of the deal: you get to live better than everyone else, but only if you play along. If you try to break rank and use your power to undermine the structure that elevated you, then you will face the consequences. Exclusivity will be stripped from you and your family, and media coverage of you will become increasingly unflattering. You will be ejected from the cocoon of privilege, back into a world full of people who know who you are but are encouraged by the system to ridicule you for falling from your pedestal. This threat of social death keeps public figures in check, and maintaining privilege while avoiding that possibility is a full-time job. In fact, it *is* the job of every celebrity. This job requires not saying anything too controversial, forming relationships that make you useful to other privileged people and accumulating wealth. For this reason, early in my career I became suspicious of fame, and more specifically its ability to alienate me from my own community.

By withdrawing from the mainstream I didn't necessarily enhance my profile, but I did develop a stronger voice, and managed to break the habit of reacting too quickly to trending topics. Getting caught up in the hype of social media is how many of us end up feeding into things we don't fully understand, so I began proactively thinking about what really mattered to me, and educating myself on it. I started listening to audiobooks more than I listened to music. I read books that weren't available in audio form, and revisited them over the years. I watched documentaries and learned about the people who made them. Before posting my thoughts, I started asking myself, 'Why do you want to share this? Will it improve anything? Have you had enough time to listen to others?' Usually, those questions would force me to save the post in my Drafts folder and follow public debates more intentionally. In the years since I started doing this, I've changed so much that I'm now grateful for everything I never shared on social media. But, more importantly, I'm also confident that my public statements hold more weight than they would if I had been playing the celebrity game all this time. If I *did* react to every trending topic, using valuable listening time to create content that rewarded me with followers for sharing premature ideas, I would be a different person. I'd feel like my popularity makes my opinions valid, and I'd probably view society's problems through the lens of my own exceptionalism, as many famous people do. If I had thousands of followers engaging with my thoughts every day, prior to developing a critical perspective grounded in collective experience, I'd lose sight of my privilege and convince myself that I am the chosen one. To be honest, I've come dangerously close to this a few times. But living in the community you serve will keep your ego in check, even in superficial ways. Like taking my nephews to the barbers and waiting way longer than promised, like everyone else. Like being educated on Ugandan tax law by an Uber driver in Kampala. Like attending poetry nights put together by community organisations, like Poetic Unity, and only performing my own stuff if they ask me to. All this provides an alternative to the celebrity world, and I get way more from it than the material perks of an isolated life.

Staying Woke

So here is my end of the bargain. In exchange for the privilege of continuing to live among the people that gave me skills, style and a perspective outside of the mainstream, I am saying openly what our music only says in code. Black life remains at the bottom of the global economic food chain. It was forced there and is kept there by a network of power relations called White supremacy. The global banking system, the laws that define and protect wealth, the Bretton Woods agencies, big trade agreements, powerful Western currencies, migration controls – these are all instruments of White supremacy. No matter how colour-blind the people running these systems think they are, the outcome is always the same: a racial hierarchy. I am part of a generation of Black entertainers whose ability to struggle with the masses against these injustices is being neutralised by White supremacist money. Not money that builds us up; money that breaks us down. This money creates cocoons of privilege that restrict our view. We get paid to reassure society that Black people are being heard and admired, yet we look the other way while our communities are being weakened, broken up and locked in more complex forms of oppression than ever before. My generation of Black entertainers has accepted the Western standard of success – material, individual privilege over others – without having a clear Black agenda. Most of us have never had the opportunity to study our condition. This makes us perfectly useless, not just to the working-class diasporas we grew up in, but also to the hundreds of millions of Africans on the continent who are excluded from the same privileges we enjoy as a result of our closeness to Whiteness. Black entertainers are Black liberals. We generally believe that society is being improved by our access to the platforms that White entertainers enjoy. We don't like the pressure of Black radicalism, because it makes us feel un-special and wrong for benefiting from the way things are. But even in the face of all these contradictions, we still have an important role to play.

3

Tracks & Records

When I was growing up, our home was a musical one. My dad, Kato Mpanga, followed my mum, Edith, in migrating to England from Uganda, bringing with him a love for music that manifested into a rich record collection, which consisted mainly of African American sounds from the seventies to the nineties. My five siblings and I all inherited our father's love of music. He invested in a record system with some high-quality speakers, and later on a hi-fi CD player that my big brother, Freddie, and I would spend hours sitting next to, soaking up songs.

Out of all of us, Freddie probably loved music the most. He went on to teach himself multiple instruments and, even though he now plays and teaches professionally, I know he would do it for free if he didn't have to work. To Freddie, music was meditation, which is why we used to spend hours by the CD player, with no visual aid. As the second-born, I fell into whatever my big brother wanted to do, and watching him memorise lyrics ingrained the same habit within me. In a time before we were old enough to have our own music devices, memorising lyrics became our way of taking songs with us wherever we went – which would serve me well later in life. My younger sisters, Beatrice and Amanda, had a similar but distinct musical journey that they walked together. We all started off dancing and singing, and we all loved R&B, but over time Freddie and I got into Hip Hop, Grime and (in my case) Jamaican music, while the girls moved deeper into R&B, Gospel, East African,

Congolese and Nigerian music. After them, our youngest brothers, Michael and Kenny, shared their own journey too, heavily influenced by what all of us older siblings liked, but mainly shaped by their big brothers.

Our parents were younger than most of us siblings are now when they started this family. My mum was the classic African matriarch, showering us with love and laying down the law every day. My dad was more laid back, keeping us laughing with his subtle sense of humour, while patiently entertaining our rambling thoughts and endless questions. It was a childhood full of happiness centred around faith and education. So naturally, when Hip Hop entered our lives, my mum didn't like it. She had always cultivated an intellectual and spiritual environment with conservative Afro-Christian values. She didn't mind my obsession with family-friendly Will Smith at around seven years old, but, bless her heart, my mum could not stand the street-orientation of Freddie's favourite Rap songs after that. Ironically, my earliest memories of Rap music come from my dad, who used to play all the hits from Bad Boy Records in his car. Looking back, I can see that he knew better than to play them around my mum. Sean 'Puff Daddy' Combs's label was a hit factory during the late nineties, immortalising the era through timeless music from The Notorious B.I.G., Faith Evans, Ma$e, Lil' Kim – the list goes on. Young African men like my dad loved this music. But my mum largely subscribed to the moral panic that surrounded Hip Hop during this time – with good reason. Rap music in essence isn't harmful, but in the commercialised form it took during the 1990s it stopped caring what effect it had on anyone. This isn't a moral problem, it's a capitalist one; but we'll get into that later.

The pull of Hip Hop caught Freddie before it caught me. I recall him listening to Busta Rhymes's 'Gimme Some More' obsessively, which took his skill of memorising lyrics to another level – Busta raps *really* fast on it, and nine-year-old Freddie could rap along better than 32-year-old me. With the 1999 release of Dr Dre's second album, confusingly titled *2001*, my brother's attention shifted almost completely to West Coast Hip Hop. Being slightly older, he developed quite a mature fascination with LA gang culture – which laced Dre's music – embodied in the form of Snoop Dogg, who became to Freddie what Will Smith had been to me. Through Dr Dre we also discovered Eminem. His music reached me via my school friend Ivan, a Colombian boy who didn't speak English. We chose each other as friends for no real reason, then bonded over Eminem's *Marshall Mathers LP* after school. I had never heard anything so depraved, but what stood out more than the madness of it was the rapper's elite rhyming ability. Now I was hooked. Freddie and I started spending our pocket money on albums and compilations more than anything else, leading to a sudden jump in our music consumption.

But outside of our home, Freddie and I faced a stressed-out community. St Raphael's Estate was a medium-sized neighbourhood in which one-third of homes were privately owned and the other two-thirds were owned and rented out by the local government to lower-income families at subsidised rates. My parents did really well to secure one of these homes, but there was no escaping the social conditions of St Raph's. I actually don't want to dwell on the community's problems because it's personal. I've spoken about them a lot, and documenting them here won't do much for the new generation but, to summarise, ethnic minorities were funnelled into neighbourhoods like mine, while White Brits moved further out of the city; institutionally oppressed British Caribbeans formed the main demographic in Raph's, and many of them didn't like

Africans. Colourism plagued our lives, as Freddie was tormented by other children for being too dark. He used to get into a lot of fights, but fighting was normal in our area, since a lot of kids only came outside to escape the stresses of home life.

I can't remember fully understanding this before the age of ten, but I do remember learning to hide things from my parents. Their worldview couldn't make sense of what was forced on us as soon as we stepped outside. When older kids would 'borrow' my bike and disappear for weeks, I faced serious pressure from my parents for 'hanging out with these boys', as if I had a choice. Sometimes I would look out the window and find one of them climbing into our garden in search of something he could play with. Once, an older boy invited himself into our house, put our PlayStation into a bag, and walked out. Another time, a completely different kid did the same with a PlayStation game Freddie got for his birthday. On both occasions, I was so stressed that my parents thought I had been part of the robbery somehow. It didn't end well for me. They couldn't fathom the dynamics of intimidation and coercion that confronted us on every corner of our enclosed neighbourhood. But I think my dad finally started to get it one summer, when he left the country for a few weeks and came back to find his car destroyed. He had left it unlocked, so with our friends Clifton and Kieran, me and Freddie used to chill inside it and play around innocently. When the older kids realised there was an unlocked car on the estate, they made it their property, vandalising it over a period of weeks, and eventually stripping its materials. I was so traumatised by these early experiences that when my little brothers eventually started playing outside, I would fight anyone for them. Still, the pressures of the estate had been a lot for me to make sense of, but as Hip Hop entered our lives, I started learning about neighbourhoods on the other side of the world that sounded very similar.

Transitioning from primary to secondary school at the age of eleven brought me into contact with other communities. My primary-school friends all went to local secondary schools, as did my big brother. But our parents felt let down by Freddie's school, in which the disconnect between middle-class teachers (predominantly not from the community) and local students (whose problematic environments sometimes followed them into class) created a cycle of low expectations and low attainment. This caused my mum to look beyond our area for a school to send me to. She discovered education league tables and aimed for the top state school in London: Queen Elizabeth's boys' school, or QE. It was a grammar school, meaning I had to do an exam to get in. I wrote about this on Episode 13 of *Have You Heard George's Podcast?* 'A North West Story':

Verbal reasoning, non-verbal reasoning,
English and maths testing.
Imagine that – ten years old working your
Ass off to make it out of Raph's, bredrin . . .

My mum obviously wanted me to go to QE
But I wasn't ready for the competition.
I couldn't even do long addition. But there's
Nothing more unstoppable than a mum on a mission.
She taught me her damn self.
6 a.m. every morning for one year straight
These times Freddie's just begun Year 8.

My mum's determination to get me into QE paid off. I spent the next seven years studying there under intense strictness, which took me about three years to adjust to. The school attracted upwardly mobile immigrants, and for the first time in my life I wasn't surrounded by the Black working class. Getting to know the Indian, Tamil, Chinese, Japanese, Korean and Jewish kids around me was a whole education in itself. We were all *from* something and, even though my parents' journey started in Uganda, I was *from* St Raph's. This was in the early 2000s, by which point the media had given a lot of these boys an unhealthy view of Black life. They looked to me to confirm everything they'd heard about the ghetto, unaware that they were initiating me into a lifelong project of setting the record straight.

It bothered me that the conditions of places like St Raph's provided entertainment for others. This feeling grew into a love/hate relationship with mainstream Hip Hop, as I was forever in two minds about its representation of Black life. During this era, two of the culture's biggest stars were locked in a feud that kind of reflected my own internal conflict. Jay-Z was the filthy rich ex-drug dealer, brazenly uncommitted to Black consciousness, and Nas was the understated but widely respected hood scholar. Both could claim to be the voice of the streets for different reasons, but I was drawn to Nas. I wanted to educate in the way that he did, as I felt more inspired by the struggle than the fast life. The only problem was, I didn't have a platform like those guys. By the time I reached my teens, though, that had changed.

Grime

In his 2018 book, *Grime Kids*, UK music legend Darren 'DJ Target' Joseph captured a moment that would eventually change my life.[4] It happened in the early 2000s, during a studio session he had with his friend Richard – who was known to many as a Garage producer and MC called Wiley. By this point, the two had been pursuing music careers for about a decade. Now in their early twenties, they enjoyed their first taste of commercial success with their collective, Pay As U Go. Garage was becoming an international phenomenon. As the genre evolved, Target regularly experimented with his Triton keyboard to find the next big sound. Eventually, he came across a setting called 'electronic square sound' and used it to create an instrumental track called 'Earth Warrior'. He knew the track was a hit when he played it to Wiley and another member of their crew, Danny Weed. They loved it, and the track went down in history as one of the first Grime instrumentals. A few days later, Wiley returned to the studio with a track of his own. He had experimented with the same 'electronic square' sound Target used for 'Earth Warrior' and found a version of it called 'gliding squares'. Here's how Target remembers what he heard next: 'Sparse, very simple, but massively effective. A four-note bassline over a kick, snare and some skippy hi-hats is all it took. It almost had a cold feel to it, hence Wiley naming the beat 'Eskimo'.' Before long, 'Eskimo' would spread, ironically, like wildfire across the UK, hailing the dawn of a new day. The term 'Grime' hadn't been invented yet, but this was clearly not Garage. It was a story with no words, and we understood it perfectly. It was like two sides of a personality. Or like walking through your neighbourhood, looking for a good time, but not sure what was around the corner. The way the beat constantly switched from playful to dark – that's how our lives were.

Me and Grime

When I discovered 'Eskimo' at a youth club, it became the first piece of music I ever wrote to. The youth club in question was hosting a state-funded programme called Brent Summer University, which offered local kids introductory courses on everything from the performing arts to event production. The scheme ran all summer and was always a highlight of our year. When I was thirteen, I took a DJ course that was run by a guy called Jerry. In the first lesson, Jerry had us mixing one record into the next using old-school turntables. I remember a room full of guarded teenagers slowly warming up and being won over by the equipment. Each of us took turns on the decks while the rest of the group gave constructive feedback. Since we were all beginners, the records were being played over and over again as we learned the techniques and fumbled through our early mistakes. This repetition became jarring after a while, so Jerry would change the records every so often. I will never forget hearing the thirteen-second intro of a record labelled 'Eskimo Riddim'. Once those thirteen seconds were over, the bassline filled the room like a wave of panic, but an exciting panic. From that moment on, my focus was unbreakable. I still remember getting an eight out of ten for my mix – the highest in the group, until another guy got a nine shortly after me. That day is etched into my memory because I knew I'd *found* something.

Later that summer, I discovered two outlets that fuelled my passion for this new sound: Channel U, a music channel that catered almost exclusively to our demographic, and BBC 1Xtra, a digital radio station dedicated to Black music. Channel U in particular changed my life. Launched by Darren Blatt and Stewart Lund in February of 2003, it was the only visual outlet for our young scene, back when TV still ruled the media landscape. If I had to pick two things that made Channel U crucial to our creative survival, I'd say that it accepted amateur material, *and* it was available on Freeview – meaning we could still access it during those months when the full satellite-TV package was out of budget. Through Channel U, I was able to keep up with the local scene. The full list of rappers who influenced me during this time is too long for this book, but a few names that stand out are BMD, who was from my neighbourhood and masterminded the North West London anthem 'North Weezy', which brought respect to our area; SLK (especially Flirta D) and Slim Dutty, who were also from North West London; Skinnyman, whose raps were smooth and hard hitting; and Choong Family, who raised the bar with high-quality videos every time they released. This was bigger than the youth clubs; people were really building careers before our eyes. For about two years, Freddie and I used the channel to keep up with emerging trends in the scene, like the 8-bar relay song format, which involved a whole group of MCs each taking about fourteen seconds to showcase their talent on one song. Classics from this era include 'Southside', a South London anthem from the Southside Allstars, 'Rep Your Endz' (both South and North West versions were cold, but the North West one is better in my humble opinion) and, of course, the all-time heavyweight, 'Pow', by Fire Camp. Yes, the videos varied in quality, but this era was foundational to my artistic growth, and the future of British culture in general.

Channel U and BBC 1Xtra are just two examples of Black musical innovation opening up new industry space, against all economic likelihood. For more examples, we could look at Jazz in Louisiana a hundred years ago; Son in Cuba around the same time; Congolese Rumba from the 1950s; Doo-Wop across the American East Coast and Soul throughout the Midwest during the 1960s; Reggae in 1970s' Jamaica; House music in 1980s' Detroit; Afrobeats in West Africa for the last two decades, and Amapiano in South Africa over the past five years. Each of these movements created new ways of understanding and consuming music – first locally, then globally. I didn't realise it at the time, but by entering the new space opened up by Wiley and DJ Target I was stepping into that long tradition of Black working-class musical innovation. Once my friend Michael gave me a CD with 'Eskimo' on it, I was set. I wrote my first lyrics in the back of a school book and, in doing so, kicked off a lifelong obsession with rhymes.

Life of Rhyme

Poetry means different things to different people. Personally, I'm not someone who puts a rigid definition on it, but I recognise that many believe verses should tick certain boxes in order to be classed as poetry. Some focus on layers of meaning; others focus on a format that challenges the writer to be creative within a set of rules. In my experience, these definitive approaches are common among people who studied poetry formally. But I've also seen those who didn't study it formally grow attached to their own definitions, which they use to elevate or exclude others. This has probably happened at every stage of Hip Hop, but I remember it in my teens, when the genre was pivoting away from styles that came from America's coasts towards those popular in the South. Gradually, legends from the West like Ice-T and Snoop Dogg were joined by legends from the East like Nas and Jay-Z in moaning about emerging styles of Hip Hop that left them feeling out of place. Although I was immersed in Black British and Jamaican music during this time, my early love for US Hip Hop caused me to sympathise with the genre's pioneers because we shared the same passion: rhymes.

It didn't take long after being introduced to 'Eskimo Riddim' for me to develop my preferred rhyming style. I've always liked rhymes that are unexpected; 'cat/hat' never interested me as much as 'surface/purpose'. I remember taking about a year to figure this out on my own, prior to the influence of MCs that would soon dominate my playlists. Rhymes created connections between words, and as a writer it was my job to tell stories with those connections. During these early days, I did so in secret, scribbling amateur rhymes here and there. I preferred ones that were complex, creating patterns out of multiple syllables, like rhyming the phrase 'in position' with the word 'imposition'. To me, these *multis*, as we called them, showed uniqueness and creativity. That's why, before our local scene took off, the American rappers Nas and Eminem were the best in my eyes. Both were experts at rhyming, constantly putting words together in ways that made them sound like the smartest guys in the world to me. But when the local scene started heating up, I discovered new geniuses in my own city.

Before long, the media came up with a name for the new sound that Wiley had invented: 'Grime'. As the artist himself documents in his autobiography, *Eskiboy*, his East London hometown of Bow became the centre-point of a creative explosion.[5] Many local legends of this era went on to become household names, such as Dizzee Rascal, who was part of Wiley and Target's new crew, Roll Deep; Tinchy Stryder, a fourteen-year-old prodigy from a neighbouring crew called Ruff Sqwad; Lethal Bizzle, who attained legendary status through Garage's transition to Grime with his collective, More Fire Crew; and Kano from Nasty Crew, whose unbelievable talent had activated a generation of younger rappers by the time he was eighteen. The wave these guys created slowly redefined British culture, one block at a time. Before long, every corner of Black London had underground stars whose reputations would travel beyond their neighbourhoods via roughly recorded demos. In my corner of North West, we heard about Roadside Gs from South, Unorthodox Crew from West, and Meridian Crew from North. They all had different rhyming styles, and I learned from every single one. But by far the most influential Grime crew of my teens was a group of five MCs from East and North London called The Movement. Consisting of Ghetto (later, Ghetts) from Plaistow, Scorcher from Edmonton, Wretch 32 from Tottenham, Devlin from Dagenham and Mercston from Bow, the collective was known for elite lyricism. In the time before I started rapping in front of others, I would memorise as many of their lyrics as possible, wiring my brain to keep up with their complex rhyming and rapid delivery. During these years, the foundation of my poetry took form. Here's one example of the kind of verses I was memorising, from Ghetts's 2007 song 'State of Mind':

Trying to change my state of mind is a waste of time
Cos I'm living in a place of crime
Where the youngers think they need iced out chains to shine
Olders on the ends still ain't resigned
I'm a owner of a skeng, baby nine, getting
Chauffeured in a Benz (I'm a lazy guy)
My Co-D's in the pen, said he's way behind
So when he comes out back to the way we grind[6]

In the space of fourteen seconds, Ghetts rhymed the phrase 'state of mind' with eight other three-syllable phrases that matched almost perfectly, not repeating a single rhyming word once. In the first line, he rhymed twice ('state of mind/waste of time') before continuing that rhyme scheme at the end of the next seven lines. But Ghetts's talent was uncontainable; in the second half of this eight-bar segment, he introduced another rhyme scheme around the words 'olders on the ends', which he rhymed with three other completely different phrases ('owner of a skeng/chauffeured in a Benz/Co-D's in the pen') – this time at the *start* of each line. So for four lines in a row, this guy had one rhyme scheme for the first few words of the line, and another for the last! What's more, the picture Ghetts painted was detailed, multilayered, tragic and profound, all at the same time. This was it. This was the poetry that spoke to me.

New York rappers Rakim and Big Daddy Kane are largely credited as the pioneers of this rapping style. They emerged in the mid-1980s, when Hip Hop was reaching new commercial heights with the success of legendary Queens trio Run DMC. The group's style sounded basic next to the lyrics of Long Island native Rakim and Brooklyn's own Big Daddy Kane, who represented a new generation of rhymers. Not only were these kids rhyming more syllables per line, but they were also painting more complex pictures with their words. Here's how Run DMC rhymed on their 1987 single 'It's Tricky':

> When I wake up, people take up mostly all of my time
> I'm not singin', phone keep ringin' 'cause I make up a rhyme
> I'm not braggin', people naggin' 'cause they think I'm a star
> Always tearin' what I'm wearin', I think they're goin' too far[7]

Compare that to 'I Ain't No Joke', which was released by Rakim and his DJ Eric B. the same year:

Write a rhyme in graffiti in every show you see me in
Deep concentration 'cause I'm no comedian
Jokers are wild if you wanna be tame
I treat you like a child then you're gonna be named
Another enemy, not even a friend of me[8]

It's like Run DMC were making a sandwich and Rakim was making a burger; they were using the same ingredients but putting them together differently. For example, the trio shouted most of their lines, while Rakim rapped almost like he was talking to himself. This made him come across more thoughtful, which people loved. Some say this was the first time Hip Hop fans started talking about a rapper's 'flow', which would become a standout element of my own poetry thirty years later.

The other up-and-coming rap star from this era was also a pioneer of flow: Big Daddy Kane brought a smoothness to the mic that you have to hear for yourself. According to Queens rapper Roxanne Shanté, 'Kane made it sexy. He just gave it class, you know . . . Kane was just so calm.' Although I was born years after this era of Hip Hop, I grew up on rappers who grew up on *these* guys. And although Hip Hop is made up of countless styles, Rakim and Kane created a lane for people like me, who liked to cruise through lyrics, taking the scenic route via carefully crafted rhymes. Don't get me wrong, Run DMC were doing their thing, but the new generation signalled a shift in Hip Hop away from the style that made them famous. On the Netflix documentary *Hip-Hop Evolution*, group member Darryl 'DMC' McDaniels told interviewer Shad Kabango that he felt like 'it was over for me' when he heard Rakim for the first time.

Personally, I've always seen myself and my favourite rappers in Rakim. He's widely recognised as a pioneer of what I call

'Reflection Rap': deep, introspective lyrics that go beyond describing a rapper's environment, becoming the window to their soul. Rakim used rhymes to lay out his thought process – from the street pragmatism of his breakout hit 'Paid in Full' to the cautionary message of 'Know the Ledge'. This approach came from a place of deep consciousness, and it paved the way for my all-time favourite, Nas. Since Nas came to prominence half a decade after Rakim and Big Daddy Kane, *his* version of what they started reached me first. By the early 1990s, when he had risen to the top of East Coast Hip Hop, New York Rap relied heavily on the new approach to flow popularised by Rakim and Kane. Nas flowed like a genuine genius. On 'N.Y. State of Mind' the young rapper hardly took a breath for the first two minutes, which made his voice sound urgent. One image *flows* after the other, rhyming in complex ways that sound effortless. Nas's attention to detail in stories of shootouts and conversations with drug addicts took Rakim's style of Reflection Rap to another level, and he somehow kept his voice passionate yet controlled the whole time. I won't quote the lyrics to his songs here. This is because flow had come such a long way by the nineties that the melodies and rhythms of Nas's rhymes can't be read as easily as the above quotes. You really have to listen to his first two albums to appreciate the creativity I'm describing: *Illmatic* (1994) and *It Was Written* (1996). Classics like 'Life's a Bitch', 'One Love', 'Affirmative Action' and 'If I Ruled the World' coded my early impression of Rap as the smoothest form of intellectualism. Listening to Nas felt like inhaling street knowledge, and from a young age I wanted the air in my lungs to have the same effect.

Coming back to my creative awakening in the Grime scene, love for East Coast Hip Hop inclined me towards the lyricism of my favourite MCs at home. I could probably fill the rest of this book with quotes from The Movement that inspired me to write; lines and verses that taught me thousands – literally thousands – of ways to rhyme. All of Ghetts's stuff was as advanced as the above, and everyone else in the group was just as talented in different ways. Scorcher also had top-tier multis, while Wretch was known for the most skilful word-play in the country. Mercston, who tended to attract a lot of female fans, was more known for showing the 'sweet boy' side of Grime (his words), but his style was very similar to the rest of them. Those four were about six or seven years older than me, but Devlin, the last member, was only a year or two ahead of me. I'll never forget hearing him for the first time on a Kiss FM radio set hosted by DJ Logan Sama. He was rapping alongside Ghetts and sounded just as seasoned, which made me feel like being young was no excuse for being mediocre.

All the Pieces Matter

If it wasn't for DJ Target discovering that electronic square sound, and Wiley using it to make 'Eskimo' and Ricky – the Harlesden man who founded Brent Summer University – providing space for Jerry, who gave his time to some restless teenagers that August . . . if it wasn't for all these people, I really don't know who I'd be. This is just a fraction of the network that nurtured our talents. Around every individual is a *context*, and a lot of work has been done in recent years to dispel the myth of 'self-made' success by highlighting that context in the lives of people deemed successful. No one gets there alone. The theme of community is a key part of this book, and my definition of it has been influenced by these experiences.

I was part of Grime's early years, so I saw it go from the playground to the world stage. For Grime kids like me, it's mind-blowing to think that right now, in the mid-2020s, UK Rap is a million times more lucrative than it was twenty years ago. This is a measure of success most people can appreciate – the money in our music propels our culture to global heights and enables artists to turn their lives around. But those of us who grew up in it know the full story – the unrecognised efforts of all those who were left behind by the commercialisation of our culture.

Following my discovery of Wiley's music, it took another two years for me to start rapping publicly, and by that time I'd improved a lot. I was taller, more confident and already thousands of hours deep into my craft. Before I stepped out as a rapper, my whole friendship group had caught the same bug. First it was Damini, one of the few Black boys in my school – a Nigerian with a big personality who I clicked with early on. It felt like Damini's rap persona came out of nowhere – witty, effortless bars that caught the attention of guys from other areas, who he linked up with and formed a crew called SUG. Then there was Nathan, the six-foot-four star athlete of our year. Nathan was another one of the few Black kids in school; his family came from Trinidad and Tobago. He was laid-back and understated, but good at everything, so it was no surprise when he showed crazy talent as an MC. Our school had pupils from everywhere, but since Damini and Nathan also lived in North West, we spent the most time together. Any time either of them wasn't in school, the day felt slower than usual, especially by Year 9, when it became routine for these guys to recite verses and draw the admiration of passers-by everywhere we went. This is what pushed me to jump off the stoop and join them.

Nathan was very together as a student, but Damini and I were a mess. We both liked to use our brains, yet we couldn't deal with the culture of our school, which made us act out in different ways. Damini completed assignments more consistently than me, but clashed with teachers and students a lot, while I was cool with most people, but only delivered under pressure. Nathan had a Spartan ability to get everything done while resenting the system as much as we did. Yet all three of us developed an exceptional work ethic as MCs. Eventually, a Taiwanese brother in my class called Jing Wei also caught the Grime bug, and set up a studio in his house. He offered to record us one day after school, so we went over, and I laid down my first verses ever. Although my clarity wasn't the best, I revealed a lyrical skillset out of nowhere, like Damini had done first. The tracks we recorded went around our year group and if there was any negative feedback, it never reached my ears. Before long, my early fanbase started to take shape across the school (especially in the year below us) and throughout my area, once social media took off. We were young and unpolished, but those thirteen-, fourteen- and fifteen-year-old listeners gave me something that was, at that stage, almost better than money: *confidence.** But more than anyone, I owe much of my career to Damini and Nathan, who not only pushed me creatively but also supplied me with the songs and instrumentals that inspired me to write. The friendship we forged during those years runs so deep that when the time came for us all to get married, Damini was Nathan's best man, Nathan was mine, and I was Damini's.

Meaningful connections like these are central to my idea of community. Looking back, I can see that this early network was

* My deepest thanks is with you guys, always.

easy to form because, being teenagers, the routine of school and neighbourhood life organised us into social groups almost automatically. Over the years, I noticed how much harder it was to form these networks as a working adult with minimal communal time. For a lot of people, moments between work are so overburdened with other responsibilities that they can't be used to reinforce relationships or unlock creativity, as we did back in school. It's important to recognise that life isn't meant to be like this. You're supposed to spend quality time with the people that make you happy. You're supposed to apply yourself to things that enrich your community. But we are made to feel like this is asking too much.

It Took a Village

Black communities are full of innovative practices that give birth to movements and industries across the world; however, these practices are taken for granted by mainstream economics because they are not seen as value-creating. This is down to racism and classism. For hundreds of years, Western terrorism in the form of colonisation was exported on the lie that non-Europeans couldn't govern themselves. This lie persists today, on both global and local levels. Globally, powerful countries like America and France claim that their extensive military presence in other sovereign nations is actually for the benefit of those countries, which are often poorer and darker-skinned. Locally, liberal programmes to address inequality within White countries often come from the racist angle that marginalised minorities need help adapting to modern (Western) society. This is the logic behind corporate-backed employability schemes and financial literacy classes, which pretend that poverty is rooted in bad job interview etiquette or poor money management – as opposed to wage theft, privatisation of public life and coordinated unemployment. The corporations pushing these programmes are perfectly positioned to end poverty by matching wages with inflation and paying their taxes in full, yet they hide behind the notion that poverty will end when certain communities get their act together.

Think about all the work that went into our music scene: the pirate radio stations that connected creatives outside the mainstream; the DJs who pushed new sounds in the nightclubs; the community workers who nurtured young talent in the youth clubs. We didn't need training, organising or motivating from the outside; we just worked, with no guaranteed reward. Now imagine if this work was properly funded. Not for the music industry, but for the community making the music. Given a society that invested properly in the people behind the sound, how likely is it that Harlesden would still have seven times the national average of people on Jobseeker's Allowance?

By the way, I get that it might seem weird for me to jump back and forth between oppression, in all its seriousness, and music, which may be seen as less serious. But hopefully this book changes that perception. Music *is* serious, especially in the collective Black experience. Our music is the ghost of our freedom and, as anybody who's ever lost someone will tell you, a ghost can sometimes be the one thing keeping you going. It's sad because ghosts are only *almost* – never *fully* there. In this sense, when we absorb or produce music, we create our own liberated reality, but truthfully, when the music stops, there is no escape. The same White supremacist horror that our music is designed to self-medicate against is also needed to distribute that music. How? The whole industry was built on old money

– the kind of money that only accumulates under conditions of freedom and unrestrained exploitation. The hateful programming that influences how Black people relate to each other and the wider world is baked into music industry norms that allow non-Black corporations to mass-produce anti-Black messages in song form. It's not a coincidence that the highest-selling Black artists of today self-identify as *niggas* but express no concrete Black political agenda.

In the thousands of years before music was commodified (as in, before it was mass-produced for corporate profits), Africans used song, poetry and rhythm to encode things that I won't explain in too much detail here. Given that humanity started in Africa, I'm not sure that peoples from other continents developed their relationship with sound or the use of music in the same way, for the same length of time, as Africans. Whether or not you get what I mean, today's musical landscape raises the same questions. For centuries, generation after generation of impoverished Black youth have led the musical world with innovations that regularly surpass their own financial and geographic limitations: Jazz from African Americans; Son from Afro-Cubans; Congolese Rumba; Ghanaian Highlife; Jamaican Ska; Nigerian Afrobeats; Reggae; Soul; Hip Hop; House – the list goes on. There's a reason why so many of the biggest White artists either directly drew from Black art, like The Beatles did, or stole it, like Elvis did. You've never seen the reverse happen. No top-selling Black artist got there by appropriating White sounds. What's even more curious is the fact that Black music has never gained popularity for one particular thing: it's anything and everything. Sometimes it's the use of guitars, as was the case with the Blues. Other times it's the drums, as with Hip Hop, or the voice, as with Gospel and R&B. Popular Black music genres come from a common ancestry, which shines through all the dirt that has been piled onto Black life.

A lot of people wrongly think the appeal of Black music comes from hardship. They say that the struggle is what makes the sound so special, similar to the way in which slavery has been used to explain the superior performance of Afro-descended peoples in sports. That's all propaganda, fuelled by a White supremacist discomfort with African excellence. I don't mean only White people struggle with this; White supremacy is the context in which we all live, and I've seen many Black people fumble through these arguments. So, I won't pretend to be above the confusion. At the end of the day, it *is* a strange track record when you think about it: due to the European control of global trade and migration, we as Africans haven't been able to coordinate our work for the improvement of our lives; furthermore, through slavery and colonialism we were denied access to education and technology for a very, very long time, allowing the rest of the world to secure every advantage over us. Yet, somehow, our music has consistently risen above these conditions, commercially outcompeting most, if not all, other forms, and creating a global dependency cycle similar to that of Africa's natural resources.

And do you know what I find most mind-blowing about all of this? The Black communities responsible for much of the world's most popular music don't live in ways natural or beneficial to them. They make this music under conditions of severe disorientation, psychological trauma, political impotence and financial insecurity.

For example, to push Grime through its first decade, my peers and I as teenagers had to move through unprotected spaces, where the stakes were sometimes life and death. We weren't the only ones; most of Grime's legends had violent experiences in the environment that defined the music. And after years of soaking up our blood, sweat and tears, the scene grew into a pyramid of un-radical content, with a few major earners at the top and a base of non-commercial talent at the bottom.

Meanwhile, Grime's musical offspring kept it moving, culminating in a wave of top-ten albums and singles over the past decade. UK Drill and Afro-Swing are two of the bestselling genres that utilised the Black community's production capacity, which was expanded by Grime, and generated millions for the British music industry. It's no coincidence that this success hasn't enriched the Black working class that produced it. This isn't *necessarily* because those at the top don't care (although yes, they don't). It's mostly because the best Black music can achieve under capitalism . . . is profit. Not change. There is no infrastructure that links Grime's commercial success to the community's wellbeing, even though, according to this generation of politicians, society finds solutions to its problems through business, not government. In truth, capitalism is hostile to any community that's not anchored in capital. And this is where Kimberlé Crenshaw's *intersectionality*[9] becomes important: the intersection of Blackness, youth and poverty in modern Britain is only beneficial as a wealth-producing asset. Other than that, it's an intersection with a lot of fatal accidents.

4

Politics as Usual

There is a political context to the story I've told so far. My parents didn't just arrive in British public housing out of nowhere, and nor did the rest of St Raph's. Our stories began in parts of the world that got sucked into the British Empire; the disastrous consequences of this entanglement forced our parents and grandparents to migrate throughout the 1900s. By the middle of the century, the empire was being re-branded as the 'Commonwealth', in an effort to make colonialism seem consensual and mutually beneficial. When the first wave of Commonwealth immigrants arrived in Britain after World War Two, they found that the ruling class here had struck a deal with the workers called *social democracy*: British elites would hold onto power by using part of the country's wealth to provide a welfare state for everyone else – free healthcare, free education, public housing, etc. The deal was heavily motivated by the spread of left-wing ideology across Europe, which the ruling class felt threatened by. This ideology blamed Europe's extreme inequality on those elites who controlled all the resources people needed to stay alive – the capitalist class. The wealth of this class, which largely funded social democracy, relied on Britain's exploitation of colonised peoples – meaning better conditions for British workers were guaranteed by worsening conditions across the so-called Commonwealth. This wasn't unique to the UK; after World War Two, weakened European states faced pressure to contain working-class dissatisfaction, but by the time my parents got here in the eighties, things had changed. Investing in the public had gone out of fashion, as politicians openly declared loyalty to the rich and contempt for the poor. This abandonment of social democracy came under the banner of a new right-wing ideology called *neoliberalism*, and we've been living through it ever since.

Neoliberalism

The aim of neoliberalism has always been to protect wealth from people power. When communists took control of Russia in 1917, it really bothered some Europeans to see private property seized out of nowhere by a popular movement. The same happened to Jewish property owners in Nazi Germany and, as calls for independence grew louder among the colonised, those Europeans fixed their minds on building a global system that would shield the wealth of individuals from the will of unpredictable masses.

Private property had basically become a religion in Europe, ever since the continent embraced a new way of thinking half a millennium ago: *liberalism*. Liberalism was a set of values that prioritised being a free individual over everything else. It gave birth to the concept of society as a collection of free individuals (in those days, White men) with natural rights who shared power, rather than a pyramid of classes under one order (which, really, it still is). In the west of Europe, these rights went hand-in-hand with a move away from methods of wealth creation that were controlled by kings and queens. Those old-school systems were replaced by new ones in which non-royals took control of emerging wealth-creation opportunities, like slavery and the commercial breakthroughs it gave rise to. This was the dawn of 'free' trade. It's one of those weird phrases that slyly means the opposite of what you'd think. Instead of meaning 'trading for free', or at least 'everyone being free to trade', the term has only ever applied to the class of individual traders powerful enough to answer only to themselves. These individuals were free to trade without a monarchy or a government breathing down their necks, controlling the prices of their goods and forcing them to submit to rules they couldn't control. Over time, the wealth accumulated by this class of traders granted to them, their networks and their descendants a lot of political influence. And in this way, Western states came to be organised according to the interests of traders, landowners and investors who controlled the distribution of wealth. It's what we call capitalism.

As of 2023, across modern Britain and much of the West, it is widely believed that liberalism and capitalism made the world better. This makes sense, since control of global trade is concentrated here. Being able to direct the flow of resources has given Europeans so many advantages for so long that many are not fully aware of this privilege, let alone what it has cost. And in my opinion, this lack of awareness – if not straight up dismissal of history – underpinned the rise of neoliberalism. The human cost of all that power has been slavery, in different forms. Masses of dependent workers have always been needed to produce the profits hoarded by this small class of European elites. Awareness of this dynamic exploded in the late 1800s, largely thanks to the work of Karl Marx. But by the mid-1900s, European intellectuals like Wilhelm Röpke, Walter Eucken and Franz Böhm had had enough of this worker-centred politics. They were more concerned with the rights of the bosses, criticising European governments for limiting the freedom of individuals to profit without restraint, as if that had ever been a good idea. They saw the masses as a liability, prone to making bad decisions based on waves of emotion, poor information and irrational desires. This early neoliberalism was heavily influenced by eugenicist ideas about some groups of people being more capable, advanced and deserving of freedom than others – like classical liberalism. Many of these guys resented Europe's trend of giving more and more sections of society the right to vote; they believed that, ultimately, people and their governments needed to be told what was good for them by the experts. But in the post-war age of social democracy, no one wanted to hear that.

Western governments were negotiating with trade unions, investing in their workers' quality of life, tightly controlling the movement of currency across their borders and using taxes to pay for public services like roadworks, energy and more. The early neoliberals wanted the opposite of this. In their view, the world was going mad by chasing unrealistic goals like higher standards of living for everyone and full employment. These guys were extremists who believed that wealth flowed naturally, so they saw any government interference in the flow of wealth as a violation of nature. Even though most of Europe shunned these market extremists for decades, their ideas eventually caught on in America, triggering a wave of political momentum and funding for the neoliberal cause.

At the same time, during the 1960s, Africa and the Caribbean won independence from their former colonisers. Well, at least on paper they did. These moments were immortalised in songs from across the spectrum of Black life, such as 'Ghana Freedom' by E. T. Mensah and the Tempos, 'Indépendance Cha Cha' by African Jazz of the Congo and 'Freedom Sounds' by the Skatalites of Jamaica. We'll look at this period in more detail a little later. For now, just know that a lot of post-colonial leaders signed their own death warrants by even suggesting that they would take back control of their country's natural resources from Western capitalists. Over the next three decades, all sorts of dirty tricks were used to stop that from happening. Eventually, the threat of Black and Brown self-determination was crushed under the weight of crippling debt, imposed by the West on the rest. This debt caused much of the migration that led to St Raphael's Estate becoming home to thousands of people from Jamaica, Barbados, Grenada, Pakistan, and even a few Ugandans.

But the 'Third World debt crisis', as it was called, didn't come out of nowhere. By the 1970s, those American institutions that embraced neoliberalism were looking for somewhere to test out their ideas. Remember, these guys believed that wealth flowed naturally, and any interference with the flow of wealth was a violation of nature. To them, trade was a morally pure way of distributing things people need, so all barriers to trade were evil. And in the neoliberal mind, nothing said 'evil trade barrier' more than government involvement in economic affairs. Remember, this whole school of thought started off as a search for ways to protect wealth from people power. Therefore, neoliberals came to see the world through the eyes of business *owners* – not the workers who make up the vast majority of all populations. Conveniently, they believed that the wishes of owners (capitalists) were automatically good for society, because the wealth they 'created' (which wouldn't exist without workers) would somehow benefit everyone. Neoliberals dreamt of a world in which all aspects of life were governed by business, arguing that the opportunity for profit would bring out the best in people. In their eyes, the government could never provide better goods and services than the business sector, because businesses were pushed to do their best by other businesses competing for the same profits.

By the seventies, this thinking had been unpopular for decades. Americans, and much of the world in general, had been scarred by the financial crash of 1929, which caused the Great Depression. Despite contributing to the crash through irresponsible (but standard) profit-making practices, the business community had proven powerless to foresee or resolve it. This destroyed people's faith in business, contributing heavily to that working-class dissatisfaction I mentioned earlier. And it was during this recession that the ideas of British economist John Maynard Keynes became mainstream. Keynes said the government should play an active role in regulating the economy, and his ideas shaped the social democratic 'golden years' of capitalism over the following decades, epitomised by US President Franklin D. Roosevelt's New Deal. But early neoliberals like British–Austrian Friedrich Hayek saw this as pure madness. Hayek argued that by limiting the profit-making potential of capitalists, social democracy was taking the West down the road to 'serfdom' – a state of bondage close to slavery. The *Road to Serfdom* became the title of his popular book, which has gone down in history as a foundational text in the neoliberal movement.[10]

Late twentieth-century neoliberals like Hayek's mentee, Milton Friedman, wanted capital (wealth-producing assets) to have political priority and legal cover that the previous generation of neoliberals had been dreaming about for years; a world where there were no taxes on the rich – because apparently this would put businesses off solving people's problems – and the government owned as little as possible, so that key industries could be controlled by wealthy citizens who would be too strong to tame by laws. This was crucial; these guys hated government intervention with a passion. Well, they *said* they hated it, but obviously, they have always relied on the government to create policies that support their view of the world. This is just one of neoliberalism's many contradictions. Another huge one is that it ignores the reality of global trade being dominated by the same old nations, companies and families that inherited the privileges of colonialism. This injustice was never fixed, so the neoliberal view of 'free' trade as a pure, natural thing is wilfully blind to the violent origins of capitalism. But more on that later.

In the 1970s, the Economics department at the University of Chicago became the heart of neoliberal theory. And this theory needed to be tested on humans. Neoliberals couldn't try out their ideas in the US because, like much of Europe, the country still valued social democracy, meaning people expected the government to stop the economy from running mad, as it had done before. So, they conducted a test-run in Latin America. Without the knowledge or consent of the continent's people, the US government started funding professors from the Chicago school to spread market extremism in Chile, then Argentina, Uruguay and Brazil. This 'Southern Cone' of Latin America was important because its nations had been doing really well under their own social democratic governments, which the US didn't like. But the people of these countries didn't care for neoliberalism, no matter how much money the Americans poured into covertly converting them. This was a problem, since by 1968 the continent accounted for 20 per cent of total US foreign investment. So, eventually, along with the CIA and big businesses with interests in the area, the US government plotted to derail Latin American social democracy through military coups that enforced neoliberal economic reforms. It didn't matter that these reforms dragged millions of people from the middle class into desperate poverty; what mattered was that a small circle of elites was able to make huge profits through the elimination of democracy. This unevenly distributed wealth was reported in the West as economic 'growth', enabling US-based neoliberal intellectuals to claim these 'victories' as proof that capitalism worked best when unregulated. This method of imposing market extremism on developing nations has been implemented on every inhabited continent across every decade since.

By the 1980s, neoliberalism had finally conquered Western politics through the election of Margaret Thatcher in the UK, and Ronald Reagan in the US. Together, the two of them changed the course of history, stripping away protections for working people that had been won over the previous fifty years. They ensured that capitalists had the final say in everything, with foreign and domestic policies reflecting their extremist views of wealth as some kind of moral authority. With this authority, the wealthy West pressured everyone else into accepting neoliberal capitalism – often through blackmail. After spending the previous two decades forcing post-colonial nations to stick to agricultural production and give up on their dreams of building advanced industries, Western powers now offered Black and Brown nations an ultimatum: bailout money for their debt crises, with the equivalent of economic amputation, versus no bailout money, with the likelihood of death by starvation. Much of Eastern Europe was given the same choice in the 1990s, following the fall of the Soviet Union. By that time I was alive, young enough to have no clue about any of this but old enough to remember the sudden presence of Kosovans and Albanians in our area. Our lives became living proof of the neoliberal track record.

From Uganda to North West

It's easy for me to sit here and break down these huge events in a string of paragraphs decades after they happened, but let's be clear: this political context wasn't apparent to everyone at the time and, because of the way History, Politics and Economics is taught, it still isn't. My parents grew up in the 1970s, when Uganda was under the rule of Idi Amin. Many Western readers will associate that name with terror, cannibalism and, of course, the infamous decision to expel Uganda's Indian community from the country. This shocking event is often presented in Western media as the racist, irrational persecution of a defenceless minority by one of the twentieth century's most notorious bad guys. But Ugandans of the time, who tend not to be influential historians, remember it very differently. Instead, many see Amin's expulsion of the Indian population as a justifiable attempt to take control of Uganda's economy.

Back in the colonial day, it was common for Europeans to import whole communities of Asians and Arabs into African colonies for the purpose of managing the day-to-day extraction of Africa's wealth. This is why Indians became synonymous with business in Uganda. Amin found that the exploitative dynamic created by this racial ordering of Ugandan industry was a barrier to national development – even after independence – and he took radical action to end it. Interestingly, though, my parents' decision to settle in North West London brought me into direct contact with Indian children whose parents settled in the same area after being run out of Uganda. These parents, like my own, also grew up in the seventies, and were only children when this traumatic upheaval changed their lives. I can't count the number of times I've watched one of them break into a smile on hearing that I'm Ugandan. Their eyes would glaze over as they relived happy memories, enthusiastically asking what part of the country my family came from. We never really discussed the politics that brought us here, just shared a warm moment. It was probably for the best; what we left unsaid was heavy with competing injustices. But to be fair, most of these conversations happened in my teens, when I didn't have the political education to fully appreciate the complexity of those moments.

Remembering Idi Amin as a monster isn't hard because of the terror that covered much of Ugandan life during his reign. What's harder is understanding his defensive stance within the context of everything else that was happening throughout the seventies. As a Third World leader who stood up to Western-backed private property owners, Amin was bound to go down in the history books as a crazy dictator. But many of the Ugandans who survived his era – albeit with some level of post-traumatic stress – now remember him as something rare: a statesman whose priority was the state, not his bank account. Western powers have always found these kinds of leaders inconvenient in the global South, preferring ones that can be bribed with foreign aid. This is why their news media keep hating on Mexico's democratically elected left-wing president, Andrés Manuel López Obrador, or AMLO, who has consistently ranked among the three most popular leaders in the world. AMLO has funded improvements in the living conditions of Mexicans by bringing the country's oil and lithium under government ownership. In addition to this, he has shown moral leadership in denouncing the inhumane US blockade of Cuba, and has openly called out US-backed takeovers of Bolivia and Peru. Yet Western media outlets constantly portray AMLO as a 'strongman', stoking fear about his military spending and even implying he has a soft spot for Mexican drug cartels. This shouldn't come as a surprise. By putting the needs of working people before corporate interests, people like AMLO frustrate neoliberal superpowers, who only speak the language of profit.

The Treadmill of Debate

Growing up, I used to hear my parents and their friends debate Ugandan politics, and on our family visits to the country I was surprised to find young people doing the same. They all argued so passionately about big events, key players and fresh rumours on the political scene, but over time, I noticed two things. Firstly, for every step forward, there was usually a step back. I started to think the purpose of these steps was to keep Ugandans on the treadmill of endless debate, not to actually go anywhere. Secondly, Uganda sounded like every other African or Caribbean country. You could swap the names and find the same story, from Nigeria to the British Virgin Islands: secret power-sharing arrangements, hidden conflicts and crumbs for the people. Along my journey, I would sometimes express this view to other Africans and Caribbeans, who would often respond with pessimism about our 'nature'. It's very hard to avoid thinking that corruption is a Black problem, when you and those around you come from a majority Black country in which the corruption is so blatant. But living in the African diaspora has given me the opportunity to look at Black life from different perspectives, and compare what our countries are going through with the Western experience. Here's what I've learned: as long as we genuinely believe that our political systems were designed to attract 'good' people and support 'good' decisions, we will continue to blame ourselves for producing 'bad' leaders who make 'bad' decisions. I don't say that to excuse us from the task of figuring out a way forward, but mislocating blame keeps us on the treadmill of debate, pouring energy into conversations that lead nowhere.

Since independence, Africa's political power has been systematically broken down by normal capitalist processes. It went like this: first, powerful companies and individuals from Western Europe and North America leaned on their governments to protect their investments in Africa. These governments couldn't be seen to be interfering with African politics, so they developed secretive ways of protecting their capitalist interests. America's CIA often assisted other Western intelligence agencies in covertly overriding African democracy by installing unelected dictators who complied with Western demands – as happened in 1970s' Latin America. It's crazy how many Africans don't know this. Foreign aid, as previously mentioned, provided the cash transfers needed to bribe pro-Western governments across the African continent. Meanwhile, the so-called 'development' sector of Western society peddled corporate influence in African life behind the mask of humanitarianism. By doing this, the sector was able to control the narrative around what is and isn't working in Africa, despite having an abysmal track record of progress. Unsurprisingly, they have maintained that Africans are their own worst enemies, but the charities, think tanks and NGOs (non-governmental organisations) that make up the sector don't put it in these words. Instead, they offer programmes that 'help' and 'teach' Africans how to do capitalism – as if the real issue isn't the poverty and lack of democracy that their governments have ensured. Again, for every African who can see this as plain as day, I seem to meet another who can't.

The treadmill of debate is mentally exhausting, and there are many who simply stay away from it, even though they remain passionate about progress. As a teenager, I wasn't one of those people. I loved to have debates for no reason other than because the sport of it was fun to me, but things have changed since then. I'm now wary of the time I used to waste blagging my way through complex issues – eagerness to express an opinion outpacing my readiness to get the full picture. If I had had the patience to read books on African politics, I wouldn't have even known which ones to start with and, for this reason, I went a long time without understanding Africa. Of course, I was affected by the frustration my parents felt with Ugandan politics, plus the frustration of my friends' parents towards their African and Caribbean homelands, as well as the absence of African studies across my whole education. All of this combined gave me the feeling that there was something wrong with Black people, and no one knew what it was. But that's the intended outcome of propaganda aimed at downplaying the reality of Western capitalism in Black life. Just like the West's selective historiography of Idi Amin, modern coverage of Mexico's president AMLO and the rise of the corporatised 'development' sector in between them, my view of Africa was limited by misinformation and missing information. Looking back now, I can see that the Ugandan obsession with political gossip is part of a much bigger condition of powerlessness. Freedom to talk about political events is the closest thing to democracy available to much of the world's working class. That talking space is important, and I've learned a lot from it, but it's still many steps away from democratic decision-making. When I began studying Politics at sixteen years old, I felt this powerlessness, but I had no idea how deep it actually went.

5

Raising the Bar

Bars

My teenage years weren't straightforward; they were complicated by my constant movement between the Black working-class neighbourhood I lived in and the non-Black, middle-class culture of my school. But amid this back-and-forth, my new pastime of rapping allowed me to hear who I was becoming. Sometimes it even revealed things I wasn't aware of, like when I realised most of my verses had a 'me, me, me' theme, which I didn't love. They either started with the word 'I', or some kind of boastful statement – normal in the Rap world, but not really me. And more than anything, I didn't like coming across as if I couldn't rhyme without stating how great I was. Other rappers sounded impressive when they talked themselves up, but I felt like I sounded childish. In my defence, though, this wasn't a 'me' problem per se. Every Rap listener knows that bragging is part of the game – the first rappers of the 1970s were literally party hosts hyping up their DJ's skills with playful rhymes about how good they were. As the craft developed on the streets of New York, Rap took on a more competitive edge, with MCs staging light-hearted lyrical 'battles' for the sport of it. This is what I was channelling with lyrics like

My first two bars will set the scene so vividly
For the next fourteen to bless the beat so lyrically
Then from a sixteen soliloquy . . . no, you won't mirror me

I took pride in having an unconventional approach to writing. This was clear in lyrics that incorporated terms lifted directly from whatever we were studying in class at the time. English, obviously, was one of the easiest subjects to borrow from, hence the reference to 'soliloquy' above. But I also threw in jargon from Science:

> Send for me, you will then eventually clock
> I won't crumble I'm not sedimentary rock

Even Physical Education:

> . . . on the verge of insanity
> I think up a new flow in the time a sprinter burns a calorie

Bringing words from class into the street circles we used to rap in was my way of joining the two halves of my life. No one likes a teacher's pet, but I created a separate category by carrying my academic clout with the swagger of my neighbourhood. Much of this confidence is owed to my childhood friends from St Raph's and the surrounding area, none of whom ever disrespected me for being a committed student. If anything, they encouraged me down my chosen path, and welcomed my lyrical intellectualism as a breath of fresh air. This Nas-inspired street-scholar persona was part of a bigger project forming in the back of my mind. I wanted to expand our definition of 'cool' to include intelligence of all kinds.

The Bad-Boy Template

By this time I'd spent half my life learning the lyrics of my favourite rappers, and I had been feeling conflicted about Hip Hop for years. The emergence of Grime gave me an opportunity to resolve this conflict by creating a new template in my own voice. And sure, sixteen years later you could say this worked out for me, but in general mainstream Rap still elevates traditional bad boys over everything else. Obviously, I never expected to singlehandedly change the culture's whole business model, but I've always wondered what makes rappers stick to the same script, generation after generation. The most common answer I've heard is that, regardless of a rapper's individual preference, they face pressure to give the industry what it wants and find it hard to deviate from the model set by commercially dominant bad boys of previous eras. On some level, I believe this. Hip Hop's biggest record companies of the 1990s were literally called Ruthless, Death Row and Bad Boy. We all have a deep fascination with danger, and rappers often present an outlaw mentality that allows listeners to experience life outside the rules through their music. But I couldn't accept this as the only explanation, since the bad-boy template was almost non-existent in past eras of Black music. Something must have happened to bring it about.

Studying Sociology around this time made me think about how humans are conditioned by surroundings and experiences. As I was finding my feet in this new subject, I subconsciously related it to Rap, which was basically rewiring my brain during this era. I noticed that many older Black people like my mum struggled to accept the genre, because they saw in it something unfamiliar and off-putting. This attitude was as common among her peers as the opposite was among mine, which made sense; differences in our feelings towards Rap reflected differences in the surroundings and experiences that shaped our lives. That would explain why so many parents and teachers couldn't be won over by the music or the technical skill of rapping in the way that we young people could. But my insights from Sociology went much further than this; at sixteen years old, the subject drew me into my first conversations about capitalism.

Self-Made

We'll look at capitalism from a number of different angles throughout this book. Forgive me, but I'll often reiterate the definition to match the context I'm talking about. In the context of A Level Sociology, we were told that capitalism is the economic structure of the world, in which profits from goods and services were invested into the production of more goods and services. Where did the money to produce things come from in the first place? That was never discussed. But don't worry, we'll get into it later. Capitalism was presented to us as common sense: if it wasn't for profit, how else would people be motivated to do anything? This common-sense view is baked into mainstream Rap and, as my friends and I worked hard to make a name for ourselves in the Grime scene, capitalist logic was a given.

As an older man, I can now see that my love/hate relationship with Rap has a lot to do with capitalism and its influence on Black art. In our ability to rhyme and tell our story, we had found something beautiful, but in reality that beauty only lasted moments at a time. When the music stopped, in many other ways we were suffering. I wanted a world in which the beauty of this music could be used to end the suffering. But I have learned that capitalism doesn't want that to happen on a mass scale. If it did, then the success of billionaire Jay-Z would be matched by the end of poverty in the neighbourhood he came from, Marcy Projects, Brooklyn – especially since this environment actively contributed to his success. But the neoliberal capitalist idea of success denies this. Remember: neoliberalism promotes a highly individualised view of economic interests, so everything about Jay-Z's journey – from the drug money he raised to the Rap skills he developed – is isolated from its social context, in the neoliberal view. The idea is that he's a 'self-made' man, who doesn't owe anyone anything, which many Rap fans believe. This idea glosses over the fact that Jay-Z did not create his environment, but his environment benefited him in many ways, like providing military security at the national level, and early exposure to Hip Hop at the local level.

No one is really self-made, but this narrative has become the focus of mainstream Rap. The same 'me, me, me' impulse that I noticed in my own lyrics at sixteen years old forms the basis of *most* popular songs. In Rap, however, it presents itself as ambition, work ethic or power. Rappers no longer just brag about their DJs or rhyming skills; they brag about *everything*. Having the most, needing the least, getting more anyway. In the last chapter we looked at liberalism: a way of thinking that has spread across Europe over the past 500 years. Remember how liberal values prioritised being a free individual over everything else? See why they call the modern era '*neo*liberalism'? Neoliberal Rap rewards individual rappers, while ignoring, misrepresenting and, in some cases, actively harming the world they come from. Not because it's Rap, but because it's neoliberal. As I was able to prove to myself in my teens, Rap can take any direction a rapper chooses. Neoliberalism can't. It makes mainstream Rap the perfect ally to capitalism because, unlike artists of other genres, mainstream rappers use the content of their songs to promote the pursuit of wealth for individual benefit.

And let's be clear: the world's richest Rap stars are not getting their biggest cheques from Black people. What does this mean for the communities that produce these stars? It means they'll never have a significant stake in their own contributions to Black culture. So, if there is a way of tying the growth of a rap career to the wellbeing of the neighbourhood that nurtured it, we'll never know, thanks to the neoliberal business model of mainstream Rap. A rapper's success usually means nothing for their community, except for the *individuals* who take pride, draw inspiration or benefit from the rapper's charitable activities. But as a matter of economic opportunity, these communities are invisible to a worldview that says poverty is just the failure to make the most of our fair economic system. And I'll be honest, at sixteen years old I believed this to an extent.

As a kid, I resented anti-Black messaging in Rap lyrics because I saw Black self-destruction as the biggest thing holding us back. Having grown up in an area that struggled with violence and mistrust, I believed that if we all stopped fighting each other and united around some common goals, *nothing* would stand in our way. I genuinely thought that our own unwillingness to co-develop a better way of life was our fundamental problem. On reflection, it's clear that my lack of exposure to Black Studies made me oblivious to the fact that people had been challenging this analysis for over a century.

The Myth of Black Capitalism

In the United States throughout the late 1800s, African American leader Booker T. Washington called for his people to embrace segregation and earn the respect of White America by becoming self-reliant. His ideas were popular for a while, but by the time of his death in 1915 much of Black America had moved on from this thinking. They preferred to fight for integration, which next-generation leader W. E. B. Du Bois famously advocated for. Although their destinations were different, both Washington and Du Bois agreed on the vehicle: Black business. In the same way that I imagined peace and cooperation in my neighbourhood leading to political empowerment, both men envisioned collaborative entrepreneurship paving the way to Black emancipation. Washington, who was born into slavery, believed Black people should make the most of the business opportunities left to them by White supremacy. But Du Bois and others could see that the lack of wealth within the Black community would always be a barrier to self-reliance. Black America had been forced into a separate, inferior economy to the American mainstream, and would not be able to pull itself up without some serious capital and the end of oppression. Still, the belief that the entire Black population could work itself out of inequality through business ownership became one of the most powerful myths of American history. Truth is, without political power, Black America was defenceless in the war on Blackness. Why? Because the same segregation that created a Black economy also kept that economy weak.

When the Black banking sector exploded in the 1920s, it ended up, in the long run, unable to build Black wealth in the way that White banks did for White people. This was because a bank profits by using its customers' deposits to loan other customers money. Those who receive loans keep the bank in business by paying back what they owe with interest and, as long as everyone doesn't suddenly rush to withdraw all their money at the same time, the bank is able to continue profiting patiently. But Black banks had poorer customers. They were poor because American capitalists forced their ancestors to work for free, their share of American land was stolen from them, schools refused to teach them, businesses refused to hire them and so on. These disadvantages didn't disappear with passing generations; they accumulated and, in the case of Black banking, they caused instability. Black banks couldn't afford to lend large sums to Black families and businesses because their customers only deposited small amounts, which they withdrew regularly.

In the hundred years since Black America's banking boom, barriers to Black capitalism have grown in complexity all over the world. I think back to my A Level Sociology class, when they told us that capitalism was about reinvesting the profits of production into more production. Remember how they never explained where the money for producing things came from in the first place? Capitalism requires capital, which, as I will explain in coming chapters, has been extracted from and denied to Black people for the last five centuries. More than violence or victimhood, more than crime or corruption – more than anything, *this* is the source of our problems. In my youth, I didn't see the danger in judging Black communities according to the capitalist gospel of self-help because I couldn't hear what was missing from the conversation. But how do you treat a sickness without a diagnosis? How do you talk about conflict resolution in the low-income Black diaspora without understanding the structural violence inflicted on it?

Crisis

In school, Sociology was planting these questions in my young mind. Meanwhile, back home my peers were making street money and, given the financial pressure we were all under, who could blame them? Capitalism distributes goods and services according to the opportunity for profit – not human need – i.e. if people don't have the money to feed themselves, capitalism will throw away unprofitable food before providing a free meal. And even though street money came with its own risk, nothing was more risky than not eating. Keep in mind, this was 2007 – the start of another global economic crisis.

Earlier I mentioned the crash of 1929, which was caused by the irresponsible but standard profit-making practices of American capitalists. Seventy-eight years later, the same thing happened again: excitement about easy profits tilted America's economy towards risky investments. This time, the irresponsible investment was debt. By locking billions of people into loan-repayment contracts, capitalists were able to profit from the interest those people paid on top of their debts. The problem is these debts were unsustainable; the assets that people took out loans to afford (like houses) were increasingly overvalued, while the wages people needed to pay off those loans lost value to inflation. But it didn't matter. Capitalists have always been bad at predicting the crises they cause, so banks continued to draw people into debt that the ruling class could pass around for profit. This is called rent-seeking, and it was far from the school-book idea of capitalism as a cycle of goods and services creating profit to be re-invested. Did debt really count? What was good about it? Who did it serve? This form of financialised capitalism wasn't productive, but it was profitable – which had been a trend in the West for half a century by that point.

As we saw in the previous chapter, the rise of neoliberalism meant no one could tell capitalists anything. America used this freedom to make money out of thin air by, among other things, agreeing with Saudi Arabia that its oil could only be bought in US dollars (which allowed the value of the dollar to climb with the never-ending demand for oil, making it hard for developing countries to keep up economically); boosting Third World debt through control of the financial institutions that lent money to developing countries; and making it easier for Western capital to go anywhere it pleased with minimal rules. These steps succeeded in bringing the global economy under US influence and, in 2007, with the collapse of American investment bank Lehman Brothers, the whole house of cards came crashing down.

Just as I reached working age, the financial crisis wiped out many of the jobs I qualified for. And in our corner of the Black diaspora, lay-offs, evictions and loss of savings became even more widespread than before. Although we were too young to fully appreciate what had been lost, many in my generation took this economic downturn as proof that we couldn't rely on the job market. Talented MCs started losing interest in music, preferring to spend their time making money on the roads. The following year, London saw its highest number of teen murders ever. Personal disagreements escalated into deadly conflicts, as relationships deteriorated within and between communities. I didn't know it at the time, but St Raph's wasn't the only part of the Black diaspora experiencing a breakdown in conflict resolution. Over the years, interviews with rappers across the world have revealed to me that this trend was a generational thing.

Former UK Prime Minister Margaret Thatcher, the dark lord of neoliberalism, once said, 'There's no such thing as society.

There are individual men and women and there are families.' This neoliberal commitment to individualism was weird and unhealthy for everyone, but for low-income Black communities, coming from the most diverse continent in the world, struggling to overcome inherited traumas of slavery and divisions created by European colonialism, it was disastrous. When the leaders of society don't believe society exists, how can the people come together?

Contrary to my early theory that Black communities would be fine if we just put our minds to self-improvement, reality presented us with a political class that withdrew all the governmental support we would need to live better lives. Like I said before, Thatcher, along with US president Ronald Reagan, changed the world. Together they pulled Western politics to the right, denying the responsibility of government to take care of its people and instead delegating this job to capitalists. No UK or US government since them has fundamentally challenged this premise because neoliberalism has been embraced by all the major political parties – even those who traditionally stood up for the working class.

What's Beef?

The recent breakdown in social solidarity is reflected in the tendency of mainstream rappers from both Britain and America to declare intense commitment to a small circle of friends and, at most, limited or conditional attachment to any larger groups. It wasn't like that in the 1990s, with the era's biggest rapper, Tupac Shakur, regularly talking about turning Hip Hop into a political party. Even in the early days of Grime, as previously mentioned, there were lots of regional anthems like 'North

Weezy', 'Rep Your Endz', 'Southside' and 'State Your Name', all of which featured ensembles of MCs from different areas. But in the UK Rap scene of 2023, rappers are more likely to express solidarity with the actual block they grew up on than a whole sector of their city. In this landscape, collaborations between artists from different areas are rarely presented as a link-up of the regions they come from. It all goes hand in hand with another trend: hostility between rappers is more likely among those who grew up near each other. It's hard to express regional unity when your enemies are local.

From my childhood to my teens, I watched beef become more and more parochial: less about personal conflict, more about where you lived. Of course, it always *started* from a personal place – fights and robberies between individuals from neighbouring estates – but the consequences of these clashes became more and more drastic, gradually sucking in whole areas and alienating those who wanted peace. As pre-social media kids, we would hear about these issues in the playground, but since there was no footage or documented evidence, the rumours would come and go discreetly. As we got older, beef became harder to avoid. It had gone from playground gossip to public incidents involving people we were directly connected to. I remember my friend from St Raph's – let's call him Az – ending up in a years-long conflict with another guy from down the road. To this day, it blows my mind that they were able to call a truce after all the robberies and beatings they inflicted on each other, with Az once forcing the guy to strip at gunpoint. I think what allowed the two of them to grow out of their beef was the fact that they were a few years older than me, part of a generation that was able to maintain friendships in areas where their enemies lived. But this standard soon deteriorated. People born fifteen to twenty years before me remember a time when everyone got along, despite extreme unemployment and abusive police. My neighbour, E, remembers the decade before I was born, when guys from Stonebridge (the council estate next door) used to chill in Raph's and vice versa. He gets nostalgic, recollecting times when 'everyone was making money', insisting that 'there was more than enough food to go around'. But by the age of twelve, I knew this to be a thing of the past. On Episode 13 of *Have You Heard George's Podcast?* 'A North West Story', I put it like this:

I wanted to hang but I noticed the estate kids that I used to play with
Slowly becoming a gang.

The gang movement came with very different energies.
And inevitably it came with enemies.
My neighbours started calling themselves 'Tugs of Raph's' as in
'Thugs of St Raphael's Estate'
This would eventually bring me problems that not a lot of
Local young black males escaped.

Raph's had issues with neighbouring estates;
Man from Stonebridge and man from MP. I
Always found this ironic cos I would've
Represented both if I ran for MP.

Before I reached sixteen, I had already been in a few violent clashes – usually because I didn't run when I sensed danger. At twelve, with my boy Jay, I fought off a bunch of guys in Stonebridge, where he lived. On this day I was told for the first time in my life that I wasn't allowed to be somewhere because of the neighbourhood I was from. Since the area was Jay's home, he had previously been friends with the boys we were now fighting and, as you can imagine, this drama changed things between them, creating new problems that would last long after the fight. This was it: the deterioration of relationships within and between neighbourhoods, panning out in our own lives. None of the adults around us had the authority (or the money) to break the cycle of tension, violence and paranoia we were trapped in. For some, the pain or shame of lost fights led to a downward spiral of revenge, which the working people of our community had little to no government support in ending.

For me, it was enough to hold my head high knowing I stood my ground, but by sixteen, as a budding artist and committed student, I would rather take the humiliation of running than risk losing my life. My area was full of wolves, and non-violence made you food. What was I willing to do to defend myself? Going to a school so far away reduced the weight of that question on my mind. By the time I was fourteen, though, Az and most in his generation couldn't fathom my age group's new norm of settling petty disputes with knives. This guy, who once made a man strip at gunpoint, was shocked that younger people in his area were so ready to stab each other. I used to find his shock ironic and a bit funny, but I now realise that Az, like everyone else in the hood, had accepted at a young age whatever standard of violence was normal in his time. If he had been born a few years earlier, he might have handled disagreements more verbally than physically. And if he'd he been born a few years later, the norms of his generation might have fast-tracked him past fistfights straight to stabbings. It surprises me that not everyone sees it like this. Some people believe a person's decisions depend completely on their personality but, if that was true, the correlation between where you were born and how much you earn as an adult would be pure coincidence . . . which it's not.

By the onset of the global recession in 2008, my community was really hurting, and everyone dealt with their struggle in different ways. I threw myself into music even more, writing and recording non-stop while trying to save my flailing grades. Schoolwork had taken a hit, since the pressure to make money kept me outside looking for opportunities. For me, Damini and Nathan, this often meant recording music in any studio we could find; we were lucky enough to have started rapping just when home studios became a thing (remember Jing Wei, the boy from my class who recorded my first verse at his house).

One day me and the bros went to a home studio in Hornsey, North London, about an hour from where we lived. Side note: Black Londoners (especially my South people) struggle to understand why in my area we're so particular about the ends being recognised as North *West* (not North) – it's because North ends like Hornsey were an hour away by public transport! North wasn't a word we ever heard without 'West' lol. The Hornsey studio was in a flat at the top of a small building. It was one of those low-key, easy-to-miss spots that seemed to be someone's actual home, but for some reason we found about twenty man crammed into this tiny space. I didn't like it at all. Londoners can be very reserved, especially street people, but there's a difference between keeping to yourself and hiding something. By seventeen, I had learned that recognising that difference was a survival skill. For all their strength in numbers, these guys didn't seem relaxed, so I couldn't relax. Bear in mind, by this point I was finally ready to accept that turning away from danger was better than not coming home ever again. But my guys wanted to record, so we stayed. Still, I went downstairs to the nearest shop and bought something for protection. I felt a little calmer walking back upstairs, reliving moments from my past that I wouldn't let happen again. And then the craziest thing happened. The mandem heard us recording and respected our talent. We ended up having a lyrical sparring session, with everyone taking turns to spit their bars. I went back and forth with a guy from Edmonton (North London) who was a year younger than me, and full of life. We'll call him S. K. During that studio session, me, S.K. and the rest of the guys all forgot about the pressures of outside, just for a moment. At the end of the day, we were still kids, younger than some of my nieces are now. Imagine my surprise when I heard S. K. got killed a few months later. Someone hit him with a brick and cracked his skull. He survived the attack and, over the next two weeks, took himself to hospital twice, but I heard he died on the third visit.

I don't mean to retraumatise S. K.'s family by bringing up this story. I ask that they forgive me, and that you respect their privacy if you know who I'm talking about. But please also use S. K. as a stand-in for every other murdered teen I won't mention. Across the community, these lost ones leave behind a deafening silence that drowns out the music we make. I remember losing a lot of love for Grime at that point. People said S. K.'s murder stemmed from a beef that started over some lyrics and, since he wasn't able to give his side of the story, I tried not to think about this too much. But I wouldn't be surprised if it was true. As a generation, we put all our frustration, paranoia and hubris into Grime, basically recycling toxic feelings to make something better out of them. Many felt this was the best we could do by the standards of the music we grew up on, but I could never shake the feeling that toxic lyrics would always leave toxic residue.

It was around this time that I started embracing my resentment, not just for the self-destructive parts of our culture, but for the conditions that created them. My lyrics reflected a sharper focus on leaving this environment, and dealing with my anger by making something of myself – *personal* success – again, in line with the neoliberal values of the mainstream Rap that we modelled our British scene after. There was no Tupac around to promote political unification across the Black diaspora for our collective struggle.

Pros and Cons

By 2008, the industry around Black music was celebrating artists less for what they stood for than what they acquired: wealth, rare items and industry accolades. On the one hand, our home-grown music scene made big commercial breakthroughs during this era, with Chip, N-Dubz, and Tinchy Stryder all seeing the kind of success that only Dizzee Rascal had enjoyed previously, albeit with a watered-down sound. But just like in America, UK rappers generally expressed little commitment to the Black struggle or the working class in general. Rap was big business and, across the UK/US Black diaspora, young people in low-income neighbourhoods increasingly believed we stood a chance of making 'mainstream money', as Tinchy put it. Looking back now, I can see that the true value of Rap music was going the same way as the value of debt in Western capitalism: down.

Like debt, Rap had become cheaply available, making bigger and bigger profits for those who invested in it. This was largely due to the home-studio wave I mentioned earlier, which lowered production costs and allowed more people into music careers at younger ages. But other than this, by 2008, the substance of mainstream Rap, like bad debt, produced little to no social value. Early Hip Hop survived on creativity and life experience, which benefited the communities it started in by organising, unifying and uplifting young people. Once capitalism was able to commodify the art of Rap without the revolutionary impulse of Hip Hop, creativity and life experience took a back seat to profit. And in an era that prioritised the pursuit of wealth over the fight against inequality, that profit motive rewarded rappers for promoting ruthless individualism.

Rappers rarely took accountability for the young people tearing each other apart within the same street culture that they promoted for profit. In fact, I'd say Hip Hop's overwhelming anger at social injustice died in 1996 with the murder of Tupac. After him, the genre's biggest stars were no longer outsiders or threats to the mainstream; they were insiders, embedded in the neoliberal status quo, half-heartedly critiquing society while rejecting collective responsibility. Rappers argued that they couldn't be expected to denounce street violence without wider structural change. Many also insisted that their careers depended on the demand for anti-Black messaging in their music, which, like the previous point about violence, has become a popular defence. And as a standard, most felt that their form of entertainment was being judged more harshly than others, like video games and movies, which also commercialised violent storytelling. In the fifteen years since 2008, I have been through cycles of agreement and disagreement with all of these points. Rappers alone can't end every negative trend associated with their culture, because the streets create the music, not the other way around. But the music definitely plays a role in reproducing the streets.

As I became more focused on creating my own ethical pathway to success, I slowly accepted the limitations that came with it. Being selective with the content of my lyrics shut me off to listeners who preferred unfiltered material. I couldn't blame them; I preferred it too, but I wanted to raise the bar.

Community

In the UK, as the cost of being alive has spiralled out of control, protests and strikes have erupted across the country. It kicked off in June of 2022, when train drivers and criminal lawyers – workers from completely different sectors of public life – called strikes over low pay and poor working conditions. By the end of the month, postal workers were doing the same, engaging in a dispute with their bosses that lasted all the way up until April 2023. Doctors, nurses and ambulance workers were forced to strike too, after the government refused to increase their pay in line with inflation. This scenario was repeated for telecoms workers, teachers, firefighters and waste-disposal workers – literally the most important jobs in the country. A culture of not paying these people enough to stay out of poverty has somehow become so normal that the mainstream media barely covered the strikes, except to highlight how inconvenient they were. All this at a time when the UK recorded its worst inflation in generations, following a disastrous budget announcement by then-Prime Minister Liz Truss and Chancellor Kwasi Kwarteng. Their idea of getting the economy back on track was instituting the biggest tax cuts in fifty years, which the government would have to borrow a lot of money to pay for. This was a budget for rich people, but it backfired: the value of the pound crashed to an all-time low against the dollar, and even the International Monetary Fund (IMF) had to tell Truss to chill, criticising the budget for 'likely [increasing] inequality' – which is crazy coming from them.

When I started writing this book, I was focused on the role of creativity in *my* community, and what it reveals about Black life in general. But as time has progressed, I've zoomed out and reawakened to the class warfare that frames the Black diaspora experience. As I touched on earlier, in her pioneering 1989 essay, 'Demarginalizing the Intersection of Race and Sex', African American academic Kimberlé Crenshaw coined a term that perfectly captures the multilayered nature of our oppression: *intersectionality*. Crenshaw's priority was addressing the injustices faced by African American women and, for this reason, she used intersectionality to explore how our overlapping identities shape our experiences of oppression, i.e. racism is one thing, and sexism is another, but the racist sexism experienced by Black women is its own thing – as is that experienced by Black men, and all other minority groups in any other oppressive contexts. The intersection of racism and classism in Black Britain means that worker exploitation combined with government neglect of public services (like trains, legal aid, education, healthcare, etc.) creates a real-life disaster for communities like the one I came from. I'm not proud to admit this, but it wasn't until I started *Track Record* three years ago that I finally came to terms with the scale of this war. The idea of maintaining a community under these conditions is insane, yet community is the only thing that will save us.

6

Black Music & US Intelligence

In March 2023, I was stunned by news that the rapper Pras, of legendary Hip Hop group Fugees, had been an FBI informant for years. I remember Pras's biggest solo hit, 'Ghetto Supastar' (featuring Mya), slapping out of speakers throughout my childhood. I didn't love the song, but my big brother, Freddie, did, so I pretended to. Prakazrel 'Pras' Michel formed the group in the early 1990s along with friends Lauryn Hill and Wyclef Jean, both of whom are celebrated as pioneers of the culture. As well as being one of the bestselling, most iconic Hip Hop acts of all time, Fugees always expressed a politically conscious, anti-establishment outlook in their lyrics. They really were the last people you'd associate with the feds.

Even more confusing about the Pras revelation was the fact it came out of a complex criminal case in which the rapper was accused by the US government of illegally peddling information about American politics to foreign agents. So, not only was Pras an informant, but the government he worked for was accusing him of being a double agent. I'll be honest, as bad as this sounds, it genuinely surprised me that none of these charges had anything to do with the kind of violent crime that Rap is often associated with. It was the most elitist drama anyone in Hip Hop has ever seen. The case involved billions of dollars in embezzled Malaysian state money and connected the biggest names from Hollywood all the way to the White House. But why was I so shocked? The idea that Rap's shady ties are limited to the streets is deeply misinformed. There is a long history of government-level criminal conspiracy across Black culture in general that runs much deeper than we are led to believe.

The Cold War: What Was It Really?

I remember learning about the Cold War in school, unaware that I was being given a one-sided story. We were told that after the Second World War, two countries competed for global domination: the United States and the Union of Soviet Socialist Republics (USSR), or the Soviet Union. We weren't told that this domination was first established by Western powers through genocide, colonisation and slavery; prior to that, global domination wasn't a thing. It wasn't even explained to us that the Soviet Union represented the East of Europe, which had been racialised and demonised by the West for ages. Of course, if our teachers led with all that, they'd have had to explain why (a) Britain and America judged the Nazis differently from themselves, when, for centuries, they had been as murderous and irrational towards Black and Brown people as the Nazis were towards Jewish people, and (b) why, after the war, the West was so hostile to Russian communists, who lost 27 million people in their fight against the Nazis. The Russians hadn't done anything but help win the war. Yet soon after this victory, America, oddly, turned on its former ally, and the rest followed suit.

Because my GCSE History course was rooted in the narrative that the Soviets just wanted to dominate the world (and therefore America was justified in feeling 'threatened' on behalf of 'freedom and democracy'), it never dealt with the real source of America's anti-communism. There was no discussion of

Western capitalism being entangled in genocide, colonisation and slavery, so the rise of communism as an alternative system was also not up for discussion. To be fair, it's taken me a long time to realise how heavily this narrative is policed in the mainstream, so I don't blame my teachers for teaching me what they were taught. But I am grateful to have entered adulthood at a time when America's role in the world is widely scrutinised. Nothing has been more effective in setting the record straight than America's own behaviour: its permanent state of war, brutal treatment of the world's most vulnerable people, non-stop theft of other countries' resources and so on.

What we call the Cold War was really the Russian resistance to America's plan for world domination. The plan was a huge project that tried to bring the whole planet under the order of the almighty dollar. This project was seen by many for what it was: the opposite of democracy. The world didn't vote for America's leadership, and Western powers went down this path while still denying their colonies' right to self-government. By the end of World War Two, the only nation strong enough to choose a different path was the USSR. Back in 1917, it became the first country in history to move beyond capitalism into socialism, when impoverished Russians overthrew their rulers in a fairly non-violent revolution. The new government had immense power in the form of a huge land mass and one of the biggest populations in the world. They committed to building a state that supported its poorest citizens, as well as overall development, by controlling the production and distribution of wealth – a socialist plan that ended up, in practice, more like state capitalism. State capitalism is a system in which the state plays the role of investor and employer across key industries. It's not the same as socialism because it doesn't change the employer/employee power dynamic, but the fact that the Soviet government was such a big player in so many important industries caused Americans (and most of the world) to label its system communist. Communism was a step beyond socialism in which most major industries were owned and run by the government, specifically to meet the needs of the people, not just to produce profit. When the government is involved with industry mainly for profit (and not people), that usually indicates the presence of another system: fascism. As of the mid-2020s, Britain and the US both have governments full of individuals involved with industry for profit, not people.

Anyway, back in the 1940s, the Western ruling class saw communism and its softer form, socialism, as a threat to the most important right of all: the right to private wealth. In the minds of American elites, both systems stole from hardworking wealth holders in order to give charity to lazy poor people. In truth though, the US, like much of Europe, also spent the mid-1900s learning the benefits of socialism. When capitalism crashed in 1929, unleashing the Great Depression on a world of workers who'd done nothing wrong, jobs disappeared, savings were wiped out and families fell apart. As the suffering of America's working class sparked anti-capitalist feelings nationwide, US President Franklin Delano Roosevelt (FDR) handled the crisis by embracing socialism. His Democratic Party teamed up with two socialist parties and the Congress of Industrial Organisations (a workers' movement) to form the New Deal Coalition. Their task was to redistribute wealth across American society by taxing the rich more than ever before, and using the money to provide a whole new level of public services, like the social security system, America's first national minimum wage and a huge jobs programme. Critics who said that taxing the rich to improve the lives of the poor would make FDR politically unpopular were proven wrong; he was re-elected three times and is remembered as one of the most popular US presidents ever. But this didn't matter to America's ruling class.

When FDR died in 1945, the determination of US capitalists to crush socialism went into overdrive. They saw an opportunity to break up the coalition Roosevelt had formed by convincing the country that socialism was backwards, and communism was just evil. This project became important to all capitalist powers. In a 1946 speech, former British Prime Minister Winston Churchill declared that an 'Iron Curtain' had shut off the socialist states of Eastern Europe from the West – an idea taken as fact across much of Western society 'til this day. But this is widely seen as a misrepresentation of reality; hostility and suspicion towards Eastern socialism were stoked by the capitalist powers who won World War Two. As Economics Professor Richard Wolff put it, 'Overnight, the USSR went from close ally to demon enemy'. This early Cold War propaganda intensified after China's own communist revolution in 1948. Following that huge 'loss', the Western ruling class fixated on portraying capitalism as freedom, and communism as oppression, which is why they started referring to the capitalist order as the 'Free World'. But no matter how big a tantrum the West threw, global power dynamics were shifting. In 1952, anti-colonial activist Albert Sauvy wrote an article for *France-Observateur* in which he categorised humanity into three groups: the First, Second and Third World.[11] He was writing just a few years after the West formed a new military alliance called NATO – the North Atlantic Treaty Organization, a powerful union representing the wealthiest minority of nations. NATO served as a clear representation of the shared interests that defined the First World. Sauvy described the socialist bloc of the global East as the 'Second World' and the colonised populations struggling for self-government across the global

South as the 'Third World', since they were neither capitalist nor socialist . . . yet. In many ways, the future of the planet depended on which economic path this last group would take. If the global South (the majority of humanity) chose capitalism, the West would be able to keep control over world trade by continuing to lock whole populations into wealth production for a small group of owners. If they chose socialism, darker nations could end up developing as fast as the USSR, given their immense natural wealth – from tropical climates that allow for way more crop cultivation than cold climates to minerals, fossil fuels – everything that Western consumption requires in unsustainable amounts. So, rapid development across the Third World was unthinkable to the ruling class. It would end their control over everyone else and force them to operate on respectful terms with people they were used to abusing. The stakes were high. Demonising socialism wouldn't be enough to sell Western supremacy to the working masses; the ruling class needed to somehow win over hearts and minds, and one of the tools they used to do this was Black music.

Black Music and the Cold War

I've mentioned in previous chapters my longstanding belief that Rap could be used for good. This belief manifested itself in my Grime years, when in addition to writing and performing pro-Black/pro-community lyrics, I would push all my boys to think outside the box, lyrically. They usually pushed back, insisting that only a narrow range of street perspectives were celebrated in the Rap world, and I usually countered that we didn't have enough examples of non-street content to judge. Deep down though, I knew they were right. Like most of my peers, I myself listened to more street Rap than anything else. What I didn't know back then was that this generational preference was directed by the music industry over a long time, for complex overlapping reasons.

Now I can see that the promotion of violence, hypersexuality and materialism in Black diaspora music of the last fifty years is not accidental. We don't need to pretend diaspora music was socially conservative before Hip Hop, but we do need to remember how radical and influential it often was. In the early years of Jazz, the genre's energetic sound and coded lyrics were enough to send White America into a moral panic. At that time, the mere expression of Black creativity was seen as a threat to the status quo. A few decades later, the Civil Rights Movement brought Black entertainers even closer to politics, although they were far from radical. Civil rights activists pushed for the basic recognition of Black people as human beings. America's absurd, brutal rejection of this notion exposed the enduring racism at the country's core. Before long, the relatively tame protests of civil rights leaders were drowned out by radical demands from the young people who followed them. This new generation wanted not just racial equality, but an end to the Vietnam war, gender equality, fairer distribution of wealth, environmental awareness and more. These kids recognised the crookedness of America's ruling class, and their music reflected this understanding. But the ruling class had a secret weapon that provided a shortcut around popular movements. Whereas activists protested under the belief that they were pressuring the US government to bow to the will of the people, the gangsters running American industry had an unelected, unaccountable government of their own: the Central Intelligence Agency.

To be specific, various American intelligence agencies came together to form this alternative government, but the CIA was the invisible defender of US imperialism worldwide. The agency was born out of the Office of Strategic Services (OSS) in the late 1940s, just as the US was initiating the Cold War. These guys were not naive about the power of Black music. In 1955, CIA Deputy Director of Plans Frank Wisner chose to send Jazz musicians over to Moscow instead of the New York Ballet, as part of a diplomatic mission to demonstrate the superiority of American culture. He reasoned that 'Our initial presentations to Soviet audiences should aim for mass appeal', and specified that music by 'negro performers' would 'serve to demonstrate the breadth and vitality of American musicianship'.[12] Think about that for a second. To flex on their so-called enemies, the American establishment sent over some Black musicians – in the same year that Emmett Till was murdered. This paradox is crucial to my teenage arguments about Rap's potential. We need to take account of the fact that American intelligence has recognised the political usefulness of Black music for a long time now.

Making America look good was just one function of Black music identified by US intelligence. There is also evidence to suggest that it was used to infiltrate youth culture and, ultimately, redirect popular social movements. In his groundbreaking study, *Drugs as Weapons Against Us*, John Potash explains the suspicious circumstances surrounding the entry of Rock & Roll into America's mainstream.[13] He points to the career of radio DJ Alan Freed, who is largely credited with bringing the new sound from its origins in Black America to young White listeners across the nation. In 1954, Freed was signed by Jewish gangster Morris Levy to work as a DJ at one of New York's biggest radio stations, WINS. Freed pioneered the Rock & Roll Top 40, a radio format that catapulted his show to the top spot within months. What he probably didn't know was that the station's owner, John McCaw, was a former OSS agent. And as a wealthy radio magnate, McCaw was no small fry in the intelligence world, allegedly serving on the advisory council of America's umbrella group of intelligence agencies, the National Security Council. His expansion of the Top 40 format nationwide changed Rock & Roll by, among other things, bringing big money into it. Potash explains that this 'dominant influence' would 'aid censorship of political songs by barring them from radio play'. So, this Black music genre, which was already being stolen and repackaged by Western businesspeople under the colonial logic of racial capitalism, was also used to silence and sideline critics of Western society.

Even more troubling is the apparent collusion between US intelligence and organised crime, which proves to be a recurring theme across the history of Black music. Morris Levy owned publishing rights to songs as well as prominent New York Jazz clubs. His links to US intelligence extended beyond John McCaw to the Genovese mafia family – the first of the mafia families to cooperate with law enforcement. It shouldn't come as a surprise that the record label Levy set up in 1956 (off the back of Alan Freed's success) was later accused by an Assistant US Attorney of being a 'way station for heroin trafficking' during this era. Freed, meanwhile, seemed unable to escape the dark cloud that lingered over him ever since getting involved with Levy. He was indicted for inciting a riot in 1958, when violence kicked off outside one of his shows. Despite being cleared of the charges, Freed was then fired and, on that same day, hunted down by a gunman in the WINS studio – apparently, a disgruntled promoter. Luckily, Freed escaped this bizarre incident, but his troubles didn't stop there. At his next job, the acclaimed DJ got caught up in scandals around the practice of payola – accepting bribes for radio play. This is believed by experts to have been a set-up, given that payola was not illegal at the time, and the investigation focused solely on Alan Freed – not the source of much of the bribe money, Morris Levy. Sure, in isolation this could all be taken as a unique story of small-scale corruption, but in the context of organised crime and covert US intelligence activity, it's worth asking if there was a high-level conspiracy to co-opt Freed's popularity for control of the emerging Rock & Roll scene – which went on to define a generation – and then discard him. This question is even more significant in consideration of the FBI's admission that they kept files on musicians such as Elvis Presley since the mid-1950s.

Tupac Shakur

As I mentioned before, by the time me and my boys started rapping in the 2000s, our subject matter was shaped by the anti-Black standards of the music industry. Is it possible that corporate control of broadcast media had, after sixty years, managed to limit the scope of popular Black music, even in the minds of young Black people? If this theory sounds farfetched to you, chances are you probably don't know the true story of Tupac Shakur, arguably the most misunderstood artist of all time. Although Tupac (styled '2Pac') died in 1996 at the age of twenty-five, his life and death are still the focus of heated debate and conspiracy theory throughout Hip Hop, three decades later. Grown men in their fifties and sixties still lose their cool in disputes over the man. Young people around the world continue to adore and copy him. I laughed back in 2014 when, after the US and the EU imposed sanctions on high-profile Russians and Ukrainians over the annexation of Crimea, one Russian politician shrugged, saying, 'The only things that interest me in the US are Tupac Shakur, Allen Ginsberg and Jackson Pollock. I don't need a visa to access their work. I lose nothing.' Vladislav Surkov, the politician in question, was reported in Western media as having a picture of Tupac in his office, next to a picture of Russian President Vladimir Putin. Even though I laughed, I thought Surkov was just using Tupac's name to make a point, as many do. But looking back almost ten years later, I can see how Pac fits among the other two names Surkov mentioned. Jackson Pollock was an American painter whose pioneering work was used by the US in the Cold War similarly to how Jazz was used: to give capitalism credit for intuitive genius. Allen Ginsberg was a beat poet whose critiques of American society influenced millions at a time when revolution was in the air. I don't think Vladislav Surkov used Tupac's name loosely; I think he was intentionally referring to timeless, politically charged American art.

Tupac Shakur came from a revolutionary family. His mother, Afeni Shakur, fell pregnant with him while studying to defend herself in what has been described as the longest trial in the history of New York – possibly, America. The 'Panther 21' trial of 1970–71 had Afeni and twenty other East Coast leaders of the Black Panther Party, including her then husband Lumumba Shakur, fighting for their freedom after being framed by US intelligence for a plot to attack two police stations with rifles and bombs. Afeni's extensive research and irresistible charisma in court were instrumental in exposing the attempts of police infiltrators to turn Panther activism into terrorism. Although the Panther 21 were eventually acquitted of all charges, their persecution was just one part of a wider strategy by US intelligence to destroy the radical Black liberation movement. Targeting of Black leaders, as well as America's anti-war left, was standardised under the FBI's Counter Intelligence Program, or COINTELPRO, from 1956 until (officially) 1971 – the year of Tupac's birth. What Afeni and her comrades didn't know was that the FBI had been using spies, forged letters and rumours of treachery to sow suspicion, and then hostility, between the East and West Coast Panthers. But Afeni was so exceptionally aware of America's true nature that if I went back in time and warned her that her baby would one day be caught up in another FBI-instigated, Black-leadership-destabilising East/West feud, I bet she wouldn't be surprised.

Growing up, I'd always heard that Tupac's stepfather, Mutulu Shakur, was a political prisoner with roots in the Black liberation movement, but I'd never heard details beyond that. It wasn't until I went digging for information that I found out he delivered political education to the poor through his acupuncture practice, Lincoln Detox, in the deprived borough of the Bronx, New York. This work was specifically aimed at rehabilitating heroin addicts and was so effective that Mutulu was invited to China and Zimbabwe to further his practice. Things got harder for the Shakurs when the FBI accused Mutulu of founding a militant activist group called the Revolutionary Armed Task Force (RATF), which they claimed had robbed banks to fund Lincoln Detox after the city of New York defunded it. They also claimed that the RATF had broken another political prisoner out of jail – Afeni's close friend, Assata Shakur. Consistently the highest-ranked woman on the FBI's Most Wanted list, Assata made her name in the Black Panther Party as an elite organiser with an encyclopaedic knowledge of political theory and unwavering commitment to militant struggle, before leaving out of frustration with the Panthers' (manufactured) East Coast/West Coast feud. After years of being imprisoned on highly questionable robbery and murder charges, Assata ended her literal torture at the hands of prison staff by mysteriously breaking free and escaping to Cuba, where she was granted refuge. Rumour has it she was Tupac's godmother. This was the family the rapper grew up in, so it's no surprise that when asked by a reverend what he wanted to be when he grew up, at ten years old Tupac answered, 'A revolutionary'.

Inherited Dis/advantage

I sometimes reflect on my own political education growing up – or should I say, lack thereof. My poetry causes people to overestimate how politically aware I was as a child, which the younger me would be proud to know. The older me, however, is just coming to terms with the extent of my miseducation. At sixteen, to overcome my insecurities about not knowing how the country was run, I chose to study Politics in my last two years of school. This helped me understand the mechanics of government and gave me the confidence to study Political Science at Cambridge, which made me look well informed to the rest of the world. But I knew deep down that I'd missed out on the real education; the one that Rastas would shout on the streets of Harlesden; the one Tupac received from his revolutionary family. Unlike Pac, I didn't know what to believe, so I gave a little time to every perspective, sometimes unaware that I was entertaining lies. My parents used to talk politics among themselves, but it sounded dry to me and I struggled to connect it to reality. Tupac, on the other hand, had a head-start in finding his political feet, having been radicalised early by the constant FBI presence in his life. Feds came to interrogate him at school about his missing stepfather, Mutulu Shakur, who had been on the run since 1981, before being captured in 1986 and sentenced to sixty years for 'conspiracy' to rob and kill. In interviews, Pac mentioned being as young as four years old when he'd hear police radios outside his window saying rude things about his mother. Painful and traumatic as it must have been to suffer endless harassment from the most powerful state in the world, the Shakurs' revolutionary struggle saved Tupac wasted years of political confusion. The same cannot be said for many of us.

Nowadays, when interviewers ask me why my life turned out so differently to most of the kids I grew up with, I start by explaining the advantages my grandparents had. Awkwardly, these advantages relate to the British distribution of power in Uganda. I'm never dying to talk about this, but it's important for us to stop explaining history simply through the actions of individuals. Colonial privileges available to my grandparents benefited my parents, which benefited me. This structural advantage, based on a hierarchy created for the European extraction of African wealth, was only available to a minority of Africans worldwide, which is why two generations on from my grandparents, it still gives me privileges over others. Whether or not Britain teaches this history in school, the effects of it are real, and provide the answers those interviewers are looking for. So, I try and explain my life to them in these terms, instead of playing into the idea that my success is completely self-made and unproblematic. Tupac Shakur should be understood similarly. The privilege of such an exceptional mother, and a life in the Bronx that started just two years before Hip Hop was born there, along with the revolutionary struggles of his elders made him, statistically, exceptional. But, unlike me, Tupac's privilege was rooted in the Black Power movement.

I'm making such a big deal out of the Shakurs because, through Pac, they offer us a rare insight into what happens when Black radicalism meets Black music. With Mutulu on the run, and the FBI constantly pressuring employers into firing her, Afeni ended up moving from temporary accommodation to homeless shelter across the East Coast, eventually landing in Baltimore. Prior to this, a drug dealer called Kenneth 'Legs' Saunders worked his way into Afeni's life and got her hooked on crack cocaine. In *The FBI War on Tupac Shakur*, John Potash presents evidence supporting that Legs was placed in Afeni's life by US intelligence.[14] Potash's evidence includes other examples of agents forming intimate relationships with their targets (as seemed to happen with co-founder of the Black Panther Party, Huey Newton), and Legs's links to Nicky Barnes, a New York kingpin whose mysterious ability to evade serious charges earned him a front-page cover of the *New York Times Magazine* titled 'Mr Untouchable'. High-level criminals evading charges and working their way into the Shakurs' lives would be a recurring theme that arguably led to Tupac's demise.

Tupac and the Government: Was It Really That Deep?

When discussing this stuff with people my age, I've noticed that they sometimes struggle to take it seriously. 'Was it really that deep?' is the general attitude of those reluctant to imagine that the US government could be that worried about a rapper. I've learned to appreciate the art of the cover-up. By presenting Tupac the artist as a well-meaning but erratic studio gangster, the US entertainment industry is able to downplay the pure radicalism at the core of his being. Since Pac's death in 1996, rappers who were in competition with him have made it a habit to pay a two-faced kind of homage to his memory through backhanded compliments and misinformation. In interviews spanning 2022 and 2023, one of Tupac's protégés, Mutah 'Napoleon' Beale, called out rapper Snoop Dogg for what he perceived as constant digs at Tupac, who was Snoop's good friend for years. In the measured tone of a devout Muslim (as Mutah now presents himself), he criticised Snoop's recent portrayals of Pac as fearful, undiplomatic and divisive. I can't lie, even I've had my view of Tupac tainted by commentary from others in his generation, like Compton rapper MC Eiht, who has spent much of the last decade discussing the man's downfall in unflattering terms. Eiht's hugely popular 2016 interview for VladTV depicted a Tupac who was childishly infatuated with gang culture and out of his depth around 'real' street guys.[15] For a long time, I wrestled with this depiction, ultimately buying into it. Eiht was closer to the situation; he must know, right? Then there were those who weren't in any way close to Pac but enjoy the luxury of having their opinions taken seriously because of their status. For example, when Jay-Z mentions Tupac's talent, he often makes sure to clarify that the rapper was not in the same lyrical class as him but commends his 'passion'. That always struck me as patronising, superficial and in bad taste, given the animosity between the two when Pac was alive – exemplified in Jay's strange decision to diss him on stage shortly after learning of his death. To this day, Jay and loyalists around him like DJ Clark Kent frame that deeply dishonourable move as something heroic done in the name of . . . Hip Hop? But few have been more reductive than 50 Cent, who, in his 2020 book, *Hustle Harder, Hustle Smarter*, literally used Pac as an example of someone trying to be something he's not: an 'Arts student' who took on 'the theme of thuggin'.[16] This might all sound like harmless barbershop talk, but it's weird that such narratives are so much easier to find online than discussions of Tupac's revolutionary significance. The pettiness of it all keeps his name in trivial conversations, alienating audiences from the rapper's radical politics.

As a teen, Pac organised activist groups at the Baltimore School for the Arts and became the youngest ever chairman of the New African People's Organization, showing a commitment to the life work of his parents. I can't judge people too harshly for forming weak assessments of the man's legacy, when this aspect of his life is hidden from view. Furthermore, for as long as I've known about the FBI's COINTELPRO, I've been mostly unaware that their surveillance, harassment and murder of Black leaders continued under different names long after COINTELPRO was ruled unconstitutional by the courts. Tupac's development as a young leader would have been easy to follow for intelligence agents who transitioned from COINTELPRO into new formations like New York's Street Crime Unit formed in 1971, or California's Joint Terrorist Task Force, formed in 1980. When trying to understand the interest of US intelligence in Tupac's rise, we should remember that FBI agents had been sending reports on his stepfather, Mutulu Shakur, to the head of the Bureau every three months since Mutulu was nineteen, according to John Potash. So, when Tupac released his debut album at twenty and suddenly found himself the victim of a brutal arrest in Oakland, you have to wonder. For the offence of jaywalking (crossing the road without using traffic lights), police officers smashed the rapper's head against the ground and beat him viciously. Evidence shows this technique had previously led to at least two deaths in

Oakland Police custody, and Potash marks this as the first of several assassination attempts by US law enforcement. I can imagine the rolling eyes from readers quick to dismiss this as an exaggeration, and I don't expect those readers to be moved by the fact that a $10 million lawsuit Pac filed in retaliation was settled by the police out of court. I was once cynical too. I found it really hard to accept that the US government was as intent on killing Tupac Shakur as I now believe they were. The casual misrepresentation of him as an immature troublemaker (mentioned above) is a big part of the reason why it can be so hard to take this seriously. And sure enough, the more negative press Pac got, the more people assumed he was the problem. As a kid, before I was even into his music, I watched an episode of one of my favourite TV shows, *The Fresh Prince of Bel Air*, in which the main character breaks an awkward moment by saying, 'I gotta go, Tupac Shakur just got arrested again,' drawing a laugh from the live audience. To a nineties' baby like me, that joke didn't sound controversial; Tupac got arrested a lot. But when you consider that he spent much more time funding grassroots organisations, performing at schools and prisons for free, housing children that weren't his own and brokering peace between warring gangs, you have to wonder why you never heard any punchlines about that.

7

Home?

Back to the Party

Earlier, I recounted an awkward exchange I had with a White man named Will, who entered a conversation between me and two Black women at a party. One was his wife, Dee, and the other was a fellow PhD student, Samira. We'd all just met and were sharing our experiences of intersectional Blackness when Will took over the conversation and expressed his view that Black people were getting swept up in a victim mentality. Before he interrupted, Dee was opening up about feeling irrelevant to the working-class Black children at the school she worked in. She described how her privileged background gave her an accent and a perspective that didn't match the Black experience these kids identified with. To this point, Samira then responded that it was wrong of people to expect all Black life to entail poverty and hardship. Samira was a slightly older woman with a Nigerian accent. Dressed immaculately, she spoke proudly of her adult sons, but didn't make a big deal of her impressive professional background. Instead, she talked more passionately about inconsistencies in the governance structures of her home country. My point is, we were having a nuanced, *intersectional* conversation. Regardless of what Will thought, Black people do this all the time. Those outside of our race who only encounter us through the media – or through a handful of relationships with Black people – might imagine our conversations consisting of 'blah blah blah Blackity Black', but that's only because racism reduces the intelligence of anyone who entertains it. Dee, Samira and I shared our unique experiences, which contained similarities and differences. This is why I found Will's arrogance so insulting; he treated us like we were one person.

Anyway, my focus here is on Dee and Samira. Neither of them felt connected to the working-class Black British world I grew up in and, as a Black person, I understood this. The Black experience is not one thing; it's everything we all go through. However, there were still clear parallels between me, Dee and Samira. We were all concerned about, if not directly working *within*, institutions that underserve Black people. In Dee's case, this was the context of her angst about the Black kids in her school. She wasn't just fretting over not feeling cool enough; she felt a pressing need to be an ally to these kids and couldn't stand the thought of losing the chance to intervene meaningfully in their lives. I don't know if every group feels like this about their working-class youth, but it's a common feeling throughout the Black diaspora – the sense that our young people may not have many chances to get life right, and that we can't trust any institution to protect them. In Samira's case, her interest in Nigerian governance, as she explained, stemmed from a frustration with leaders detached from the suffering of the masses, and systems that seemed designed not to work. This is not an exclusively African problem, as our earlier look at strikes across the UK showed us, but it is a general norm across Black life, with extreme consequences for hundreds of millions of people. Conversation between the three of us flowed so organically because we were all committed to some sort of social responsibility towards our own. I can't speak for Dee or Samira, but personally I've always used socially motivated work to express love for the place I call 'home'.

Still, towards the end of my teens, as my time in the Grime scene drew to a close, I became more and more frustrated with our community. On the one hand, my network had expanded through music, which I was grateful for, because I was surrounded by talented MCs everywhere I went, but on the other hand, it felt like too many young Black males in our circle were getting caught up in street problems. We had to be mindful of the studios we recorded in and the politics between people we were connected to. By the time I was nineteen, years of navigating this space just to make music started to take a toll on me. I was jaded. Having recently secured a place to study Politics, Psychology and Sociology at the University of Cambridge, I was ready to move on to a new challenge.

Home Home

During this time, I took my first ever break from education in the form of a five-month trip to Uganda. I talked about this turning point on Episode 23 of *Have You Heard George's Podcast?* 'Back to UG':

> My mum suggested that I take some time to
> Unwind before the Cambridge grind.
> So, I spent half a year in Uganda
> And it changed my life . . .
>
> While I was out there, I thought about the ends,
> The lifestyle claiming all my childhood friends.
> I wished I could fly the whole hood to Uganda,
> Just walk around with them, absorb the powers dem.

Don't get me wrong – in Ugandan society there's all sorts of malcontent.
There's greed, corruption, people starving,
But even the orphans in the streets were laughing.

I can't explain it.
Fifty years before, the country never even existed.
The British forced all these kingdoms together,
And a whole lot of people resisted.
By 2010, Uganda was popping.
When I came back people thought man had a problem.
I was down in the dumps. Cos I caught feelings for the country
After living there for how many months.

For years, I struggled to explain why that trip had such a huge impact on me. Every time I tried, my reasons changed. I said it was because I saw so much happiness on so many faces, or because of the sun, or because Ugandans were always partying. And it's true; I loved the weather, I met more polite, fun-loving people than I'd ever met in my life, and I laughed hard every day – Ugandans love to laugh. But the country wasn't perfect, as I learned from the daily mistreatment and injustices that Ugandans put up with. Bribes and shortcuts were part of every system, and you had to constantly beware of unexpected health and safety hazards. So why did I love this place so much?

To be honest, the Ugandans I met were just nicer than what I was used to. For example, where I grew up, if you stopped a random brother and asked him for directions, you could never be sure how he'd react. He could help out with no qualms, or close up and give you the feeling that you shouldn't be around here. But in Kampala, the capital city in which I spent most of my time, when you stopped a young man for directions, no matter how rough, or tired, or hungry he looked under the blazing sun, he would always compose himself and greet you formally. His demeanour would be unassuming, and in his eyes you'd almost never see that defensiveness that was standard back in St Raph's. Yet more often than not, his situation looked harsh. I used to ask for directions from a young street vendor or a *boda-boda* driver. *Boda-bodas* are motorbike taxis that flooded the country in the early 2000s. Due to half-hearted law enforcement, many *boda* drivers barely had a licence, having come from the village to find steady employment in one of the country's few reliable industries – transport. These guys spent their time waiting outside busy buildings and shuttling passengers across the city's messy roads. They haggled all day because there were no fixed rates. And no matter how hot or rainy it was, they were forced to stay outside, otherwise they wouldn't eat. The street vendors had it even worse. They were usually posted by busy traffic lights carrying a million random items, hoping to find a buyer in the dense traffic. Chewing gum, fruits, toys – these young men and women would sell whatever they could get their hands on, often competing with begging, dusty children for a driver's attention. Their lives seemed highly stressful, but for some reason I never saw them give anyone attitude. I'm talking about young people, who were forced to risk their safety on Kampala's crazy streets every day, with no financial safety nets. How could they stay so level-headed? I mean, 'level-headed' is an understatement; you could often see them lounging and joking with their friends on the roadside before putting on a business face for customers. It's like they had an internal latch that would stop them from flying off the handle.

I noticed this sense of restraint across many aspects of Ugandan behaviour. Road rage was way more justifiable but much less common in Kampala than in London. When cars knocked into each other, people would honk their horns, mildly irritated, then move on. In London, I regularly saw worse happen over less. Ugandans were constantly cheating each other out of money, but their threshold for violence was way higher than what I was used to. I even saw restraint in how they dealt with tragedy. People often told me heart-breaking stories about losses and traumas in their lives, but they did so with a smile. In Kampala, it was normal to hear of someone raising their siblings after their parents died, or working to put themselves through school because they had no support. Yet, if they did harbour any bitterness, they hid it well. This was different to the environment I was used to, where early childhood traumas often caused people to spiral out of control. Funnily enough though, what I found most amazing was the lack of drama in the club. For a social scene that was known for drinking and casual sex, Kampala night life wasn't anywhere near as messy as it could have been. I don't think I saw one fight throughout my first trip, and by this time, the London club scene was increasingly unpredictable. These contrasts played on my mind. Why were young Ugandans so much calmer than their counterparts in Britain?

I could have been wrong, but I felt it was because Ugandans valued their place in society more. No matter how poor or stressed they were, they didn't seem to feel like outlaws in the way that so many of us did in Black Britain. This is why street kids in Kampala greeted strangers formally, and why petty arguments didn't routinely end up in casualties. The more I thought about it, the more it made sense. Ugandans were living in the country their ancestors had inhabited since the beginning of humanity – no amount of corruption or poverty could change that. And, as frustrating as the country's broken systems could be, in Uganda I saw people who behaved like they belonged. This is what was missing in our lives. No matter how politically stable the UK was, the community remained insecure. Unlike Ugandans, we had no shared history that rooted us in cultures designed to protect us. We were on our own. Don't get me wrong, I'm not saying all indigenous populations necessarily feel secure in their homelands, but Ugandan people definitely had a live-and-let-live vibe about them. It's what allowed me to move through the country unaccompanied for five months, no wahala. Maybe it helped that I was young, Black and male, but given that these factors often led to me being treated with suspicion in London, I welcomed the opportunity to blend in. And this brings me to the second reason why I loved Uganda.

For the first time in my life, race wasn't a factor. As I slowly adjusted to the freedom of not seeing myself through European eyes, I came to realise that 'Black' was a separate category to 'African'. This made me think differently about the problems faced by my peers back home. It made sense that Grime often sounded angry, whereas Ugandan music was usually happy. It made sense that young Black men in London were wary of each other, knowing we could be victims of violence just for looking alike, while our brothers in Kampala treated each other better under harsher conditions. It made sense that our families and communities were often divided in Britain, while our counterparts in the motherland commonly shared responsibility for each other's children, and were more likely to collectively care for their elderly. And in a twisted way, it even made sense that the abuse of Black women was normalised in diaspora music, whereas, for all its problems, Africa produced music that celebrated women. Up to this point I had never considered living anywhere other than North West London, but Kampala was making me a better offer.

8

Changes

After returning from Uganda to the UK, I quickly realised how much the urban music scene had changed. Grime was fading and a new form of Rap was emerging. 'Road' Rap was a slower, less teen-dominated subgenre of UK Rap, spearheaded in South London by a Peckham artist called Giggs. It's funny how one voice can move a generation. Years of making music while running the streets hadn't been lucrative for Giggs until his breakout record 'Talkin' Da Hardest' took over the underground Rap scene, then eventually the mainstream. His style was completely original: where most Grime MCs sprinted through their lyrics, Giggs jogged and sometimes even walked. Where most MCs talked hypothetically about what they *could* do, Giggs talked brazenly about what he was known for. Most MCs painted over-the-top pictures of themselves, but Giggs gave you a down-to-earth depiction of his whole landscape: the politics of his area; the hierarchy of his team; the complexity of his feelings. Also, Giggs was older than the average MC. Grime had become overrun with teenage rappers who ran lyrical circles around each other, but when Giggs blew up the culture shifted. His story travelled as far as his music and, in the pre-Instagram era of the late 2000s, when even YouTube wasn't part of everyday life, underground artists could remain faceless for a long time, which made Giggs seem mysterious and unreachable. We heard he ran Peckham. We heard he got locked up for firearms. We heard the police hated him. These rumours became as big as his most popular songs, and within two years, Giggs's deep voice could be heard playing from the phones of teenagers all over the city. They didn't care that their speakers made the music sound tinny and annoying to everyone else – to be fair, most of Giggs's songs weren't professionally recorded anyway. It wasn't about sounding clean and polished – it was about being heard. Giggs brought a new audience closer to the streets than ever.

As a Rap fan, I wasn't immune to the Giggs hype, but as an MC, I was happy to bow out. I read the room and figured there was no more space for a non-gangsta Grime lyricist like me. And so, for the first time in four years, I stopped actively pursuing a music career. Still riding high from the spiritual refill that Uganda gave me, I was happy to quietly start my degree at Cambridge and put all that music stuff to one side. Or so I thought.

Then I Got into Cambridge

At the start of October 2010, my dad and I packed my belongings into his van and, along with my mum, we headed off to my new university. This was one of the proudest moments of my life, and I was grateful to be sharing it with my parents. It wasn't always clear that I would make it this far, though. Three years prior, I had earned GCSE grades that I myself couldn't believe, given how distracted I was with my budding Grime career at the time. But not long after that, my . . . *relaxed* approach to studying threw my mum into a panic when my first A Level results came in and I got a D and an E in History and Politics. My English results were alright – I got a B, but only because I did really well in one paper and not so well in another.

None of this was a surprise to me – like I said, my unexpected GCSE results were the real shock. In honesty, I hated school, but I hated losing even more, and that's the only thing that kept me on that A Level course. Deep down, I was more interested in making music and making money – all my spare time was spent on these two activities.

Before I turned sixteen, because I couldn't be formally employed, I used to hustle, working for tips as a runner at the barbershop, and selling any clothes, phones or tickets I could get my hands on. But once I turned sixteen, I qualified for legal work, and quickly got my first job at a local call centre. That place attracted young people from all over the area, and I loved it. It was exciting to move into this professional world where everyone looked and smelled good. The problem was, I could only get shifts after school. So, as soon as my last lesson was over, I would make that hour-and-a-half trek from Arkley to Stonebridge Park, then start a four-hour shift. My mum was against this. She knew I loved earning and if this job clashed with my studies, I'd never admit it. We argued a lot over that call centre but, as she predicted, I wasn't giving it up for nothing. So, you can imagine her rage when my exam results exposed exactly how distracted I truly was. I made excuses about adjusting to my new surroundings but generally, it continued like that for the next two years. This is probably why some of my teachers were less than confident in my plan to apply for Cambridge. But one teacher had no doubts about me – probably because her subject captured my imagination.

Nisha Manoharan was my Sociology teacher. She was fresh out of university, with a calm, friendly energy, and was so ahead of her time that the first homework she ever gave us was to watch David Simon's *The Wire*. This was in 2007, when most of the world was still sleeping on the show, which is now widely recognised as the greatest in TV history. Ms Manoharan told us that *The Wire* was the perfect introduction to Sociology, and I ignored her because homework that couldn't be marked wasn't homework to me. Big mistake. When I finally got around to watching the show years later, I realised that not only was she right, but I would have grown so much as a human being if I'd watched it when she told us to. Ms Manoharan covered one half of our Sociology course, but the other half was taught to us by Tahmer Mahmoud, another new teacher. Just like Ms Manoharan, Mr Mahmoud was young, likeable and sharp. He also made Sociology relatable by talking us through the subject, using analogies from sports and popular culture to open our minds and provoke critical thinking. When I got my B, D and E in English, History and Politics, I also got an A in Sociology. Honestly, I can't remember ever getting less than an A in the subject – I liked it, and it seemed to like me. By giving me the tools to understand the systems that shape our behaviour, Sociology became relevant to my personal life. In English we studied dead writers, in History we studied dead leaders and in Politics we studied both, but Sociology was the only subject that talked about *us* – all of us. It dealt with school, family, crime – things that were alive in my life at the time. I could take the ideas it gave me and use them to understand my surroundings, which I couldn't do with any other subject. And at that point in my life, I was desperate to understand. So, when I told Ms Manoharan that I wanted to study Sociology at Cambridge, she was immediately supportive. She'd studied there herself and recommended that I apply to the same college she went to – King's.

Fast-forward to October 2010 and there I was in the van with my parents, on the way to King's College, Cambridge. I had retaken some exams and applied for university one year later than my friends for a better shot at making it – all my mum's idea. After my Head of Year discouraged me from submitting a Cambridge application, my mum went to the school and fought my case, which made me uncomfortable because the teacher had me convinced that Cambridge was out of my reach. For these reasons, making that trip up to Cambridge with my parents was extra special. Once I settled into my new accommodation, I met my nearest neighbours – a sweet Japanese girl called Yuho, and a charismatic mixed-race guy called Ricky. Yuho was on the same course as me, but Ricky was studying Natural Sciences. There was another Asian student on our floor, but he was quiet and reserved, so I never got to know him. I'm not sure how Yuho remembers it, but she soon became my guardian angel for all things related to our course. Since we lived next door to each other, we'd often meet up in the kitchen, where she would ask how I was getting on with an essay, and I'd be like '. . . Which essay?' She'd patiently bring me up to speed on whatever email I hadn't read or whatever lecture I'd missed, and she'd even lend me her notes if I had none. I definitely owe some of my first-year grades to that girl. Yuho, wherever you are, thank you! Ricky was actually the first person I spoke to when I moved in. If I remember correctly, he was part South American and part Asian, but talked with that American accent all international students had. We clicked. He had this grin that made everything seem like a joke or an adventure, and he was easy-going. In my three years at Cambridge, I don't think I heard Ricky say one bad thing about anyone. Coming from such a multicultural environment as London, it took me a while to notice that our whole floor was the only one throughout the entire college with no White students.

The university was made up of campuses called colleges, and each one had its own culture. King's was known for having the highest proportion of students from state schools out of all the Cambridge colleges. This was partly why Ms Manoharan recommended it to me; the culture of your college basically defines your Cambridge experience. During my first term, I threw myself into the King's social scene. It didn't take long for me to learn that Cambridge did a lot of things differently to most universities – like starting in October while everyone else kicked off in September, or allowing just a few days to celebrate the arrival of new students, whereas my friends in other universities enjoyed a weekend-to-weekend party known as 'Freshers Week'. Over those first few days we mingled by the student bar and got to know each other at drink-ups in different dorms. After that, there were weekly dinner parties called 'formals' and I tried to attend every one. At the time, it was generally accepted that the local club scene wasn't great, with DJs playing a genre I'd never heard of – 'Cheese'. This wasn't a real genre, just the name given to the cheesy songs that were common in Cambridge nightlife; I remember once hearing the opening soundtrack of *The Lion King* at around 1 a.m. That was crazy. None of this bothered me too much though, since I came for the education, not the nightlife. To be honest, part of me was still in disbelief that I'd actually made it here. It was ranked the best uni in the world. Fifteen thousand people applied that year, and fewer than four thousand of us got in. Dozens of people applied for my specific course via my specific college, and I was one of the ten or so who were admitted. Sometimes I thought about those odds and felt funny. Most of my childhood friends barely reacted when I told them I was going to Cambridge because they didn't really know what it was. They were just proud of me for going to university, period. They didn't know I was constantly fighting the feeling that I'd cheated the system, like one day I was going to slip up, and fail so hard that everyone would realise I wasn't supposed to be there. Looking back, I can see that this feeling was linked to the fact I was the only Black guy on campus.

Then I Wasn't Around Black People

Strictly speaking, I was the only Black male *in my year* at King's. There was also a mixed-race sister, one Black male in the year above us and another in the year above him. Out of the 710 students on campus, the four of us didn't establish much of a presence. We barely saw each other, which was normal in such a work-intensive place. But even if we had seen each other more, we were different personalities from different backgrounds, so it was understandable that we didn't automatically form a friendship group. At first, I didn't think much about the lack of Black people, or how it affected me. Beyond my college life, I'd joined the university's African Caribbean Society, which was headed by my old friend, a British Bajan and Jamaican brother called Kalil. In fact, the last time I was in this situation, Kalil was right there with me. We met in Year 7 as two of the three Black boys in our class – all three of us making up one-third of the nine Black pupils in our year. Whereas I was a half-hearted student, Kalil was always a model student and a promising athlete. I can't remember a single subject he wasn't in the top set for, and as if that wasn't enough, he played like two or three instruments at a high level. In fact, when our Head of Year was discouraging me from applying to Cambridge, he was supporting Kalil's application at the same time. Since I took my turn a year later, I told Kalil in secret, and he quietly supported me the whole way. Now studying Law at Jesus College, Cambridge, it made sense that Kalil was the ACS President. In this role, he made it his business to welcome all new members of the ACS with a showcase celebrating the cultures and talents that we brought to Cambridge. *Culture Fest 2010*, as he called it, was scheduled for the end of October, and Kalil wasted no time in recruiting freshers. Knowing my background as an MC, he came straight to me.

'Nah, I'm cool,' was my immediate response when Kalil asked me to perform at his upcoming talent show. He looked stunned. The guy had seen me go from zero to a hundred as a Grime MC over the previous four years. When we met as eleven-year-olds, we both loved to perform – sometimes we even competed, doing Michael Jackson covers. But by our mid-teens, Kalil had watched me completely reinvent myself. He couldn't fathom how I could go from writing lyrics obsessively in the back of every class, and practising with the mandem every break, every lunchtime, every bus journey, to now just: 'Nah, I'm cool'. I didn't know how to explain to him that I was over it. Apart from the fact I hadn't written anything in about a year, all of my old verses were tied to the environment I'd just left behind. My slang, my concepts, my whole style of writing came from Grime culture, but this was Cambridge University, where (at the time) I could probably count the number of Grime fans on one hand. I had always known this culture as something created and consumed by Black boys in our natural environment. The thought of bringing it to a hall full of stiff academics who likely wouldn't even catch what I was saying made me cringe.

I managed to explain this much to Kalil, but I held back the deeper reason why I didn't want to perform. Truthfully, I was intimidated. The burden of representing our culture to a world that looked nothing like us was a lot. I'd just got here; what if they all started being weird with me because I'd shown them too much too soon? What if my 'normal' was so different to theirs that they couldn't be honest with me about how they really saw me? I didn't say all this to Kalil, but he's a smart guy, and I'm sure he sensed my discomfort. Luckily for both of us, it wasn't his style to take no for an answer, especially when he believed in something. He chased for weeks until I finally thought of a compromise: I would perform an acoustic set of fresh material. None of my old lyrics, no Grimey instrumental tracks that would overpower my voice. Just me and a piano, or a guitar or something. Kalil was happy with this compromise and, in that moment, the seed of my poetry career was planted.

It's crazy how a change of environment can affect your options. Whenever I reflect on my first month of Cambridge, I'm reminded that I might never have come to poetry if I didn't feel so uncomfortable at the time. This feeling forced me to reinvent my presentation, and suddenly, four years of Grime became all the training I needed to start something new. Since sixteen, I'd had the idea that Grime without music was poetry. This idea came from a talent show I performed at when the sound cut out and I had to rap with no music and no microphone. I believed in what I was saying so much that the audience blessed me with a standing ovation. Not long after, a trusted friend called Sandra backed up my idea that Grime was close to poetry. I used to practise my lyrics on the phone to her, and one day she pointed out that this delivery was unique. She said that without the instrumental, my words stood out even more. Her consistent (sometimes brutal) honesty gave me no reason to doubt her, which is one of the reasons why we eventually got married. But back then, Grime was the love of my life, and the kind of Grime my friends and I were most obsessed with was clever and layered. MCs like Kano and Ghetts were known for complex rhyme schemes that you couldn't even rap along to without daily practice, while Wretch 32 was the ultimate street poet. He told deep stories and used understated wordplay that sometimes took me years to decode. Then there was Skepta, whose creativity was endless. Like most MCs, Skepta had a boisterous persona that was entertaining in itself, but his lyrics were skilful, empowering and funny – so, so funny – especially when he was clashing someone, which he always was. Between 2006 and 2009, both the number of MCs and the quality of writing across my demographic shot up, mainly because of the guys I just mentioned. This kept me competitive. I would write and practise everywhere. I woke up with lyrics in my head. I took it personally when someone was further on than me. I wanted every power available to an MC – speed, flows, wordplay – everything. But by far, my true strength was storytelling, and being in Cambridge pushed me to build on this.

Then I Found a New Audience

When Kalil finally persuaded me to perform at *Culture Fest*, I was still enjoying Cambridge. I saw it as a dream that became a reality and, believe it or not, it had seemed like more of a longshot than my dream of making it as an MC. Because of the dedication and creativity that music unlocked within me, I was convinced at one point that I could make it big. However, I was less confident about taking my education this far; I just didn't enjoy it as much. So, this period of my life was surreal, because one dream was overtaking the other. What's more, between the two of them, Cambridge was actually the *secret* dream. Everyone knew me as an MC, but no one knew I was applying for this uni, and I'm sure most of my MC friends didn't even know I was academic like *that*. But Kalil was right – I had worked too hard at music to just let it go. Yeah, the shift in the streets from Grime to Road Rap wasn't for me, but Cambridge wasn't the streets. In fact, nothing was the streets apart from the streets, so why would I let the streets dictate what I did with my art? With my story? I told myself it was time to test out this theory of Grime passing for poetry. No one would give me permission to do what I saw in my mind, so what was I waiting for? I knew how performance worked: *remove any barriers between you and the audience and give them energy*. If I stuck to these principles, I couldn't fail. I thought back to the years I'd put into Grime and rediscovered my confidence. Nothing was more nerve-wracking than the first time I performed publicly, and I survived that. Not only did I survive – I rose to the top of my local scene. Except for one of my childhood friends (who laughed in my face when he first heard me rap because the transition was too weird for him) no one ever rejected me as an MC.

When *Culture Fest* finally came around, my nerves were working overtime. I had written two fresh pieces with language, content and delivery adjusted for my new audience. These pieces were heavily influenced by an upcoming South Carolina rapper called J. Cole. It had been a long time since US Hip Hop dominated my playlist, but this was a season of change. While the American Rap market had been cornered by traditional gangstas like 50 Cent and Young Jeezy during the previous decade, it was now developing a taste for new perspectives, thanks largely to the influence of Kanye West. I related to J. Cole; he was a good kid from a ghetto area with more conscious verses than the average rapper. A scholarship to St John's University took him to New York City, but Cole intended for this move to also bring him physically closer to a record deal in the home of Hip Hop. J. Cole's lyricism and pan-African worldview gave me what most Rap and Grime couldn't at the time. I was fascinated by his stories about adjusting to university life while pursuing a Rap career, and I wrote along those lines.

The week before my *Culture Fest* performance, I met a tall, friendly guitarist called Isaac. I told him my idea of rapping in a more laid-back, poetry-kind-of-way, and he was interested. Since I wasn't a musician, I used other people's music to give Isaac an idea of what I wanted, and the best example of a guitar line that I could rap to was the instrumental of 'I Got a Story to Tell' by Biggie. Isaac listened to this and came up with his own riff. Because of the time I'd lost telling Kalil I wouldn't perform, we didn't have long to practise, which was weighing on my nerves along with the fact I hadn't rapped publicly in about a year. But I couldn't back out. The night of the showcase arrived and, after a string of talented singers, comedians and other poets, Isaac and I stepped onstage. All I remember is blurting out an awkward introduction with a joke that didn't land well before Isaac started playing. I got into the rhythm, tried to ignore the faces in front of me, suppressed the sickness in my stomach and spoke my truth.

PART II

The Short Run

9

Zooming Out

Around the same time as my *Culture Fest* performance, French secret agents were launching an operation in one of Africa's most powerful countries. That country was Libya, and when I think about what happened next, I struggle to believe how naive I was.

Gaddafi, France and Africa

Libya is an oil-rich nation in North Africa – the fourth biggest on the continent – with a mostly Arab population. In 1969, the country's King Idris was overthrown in a coup led by a young colonel called Muammar Gaddafi. Over the following decades, Gaddafi kept a firm grip on power, maintaining an anti-Western stance that was expressed in overt and covert militarism. To summarise a long and complex history, Libya's massive oil reserves combined with its anti-colonial leadership kept the country politically independent, relative to others across the Arab world and the African continent. Gaddafi was viewed in the West as a crazy dictator, while his reputation for solidarity with Africans reached far and wide (though it was made complicated by his interference in the affairs of other African nations). I didn't know any of that growing up, but by the time I'd caught up on this chapter of history, things had changed dramatically. What happened to Libya in my twentieth year of life set off a chain of events so damaging to Africans that it eventually shifted the focus of my career.

Just months before the West's 2011 invasion of Libya, Gaddafi urged his African and Muslim allies to unite and embrace a new currency: the gold dinar. This currency would be backed by actual gold, which the Libyan leader was believed to have stored away in serious amounts. Since becoming president of the African Union in 2009, Gaddafi proposed the adoption of this African currency, arguing that it would end the domination of the almighty dollar and, in doing so, free the continent from European oppression.

To me, the most mind-blowing example of this oppression is the control France exerts over the currencies of fifteen African countries. The French treasury sets the value of these currencies, and France's government has been known to lower that value overnight without notifying a single African head of state. The Africans are not allowed to handle foreign currency without France's permission. Their foreign currency savings are held in French banks and invested in whatever the French want, without their permission. They have to check in every single day to let France know how much they have made, or how much they need. Their coins and notes have been manufactured in France this whole time. And Gaddafi had a plan to end all that. This is why in 2011, during my first year of university, French president Nicolas Sarkozy labelled Libya a 'threat to the financial security of mankind'. Gaddafi called on African and Muslim nations to sell their oil and natural resources in gold dinars only, which would have made the dollar and the euro redundant.

As a teenager, none of this information reached me. In fact, aside from my time in Uganda, I basically knew nothing about Africa. There's a reason why this lack of self-knowledge didn't stop me from getting into one of the 'best' universities in the world: 'successful' members of the diaspora are not *required* to understand or even think about Africa. Therefore, as Western news outlets framed Libya being dragged to hell as a humanitarian victory, I had no idea we were witnessing the denial of African self-determination in real time. In order to develop any insight into African affairs, I'd have to be in circles that proactively analysed African issues from an African perspective, which I wasn't. And honestly, I don't think much of the diaspora was either. Black people in the West are educated according to Western national curricula, with little to no focus on the parts of the world we come from. Furthermore, Western school systems tend not to look at modern Black life in any in-depth way and, for this reason, many of us grow up with huge gaps in our understanding of the politics that affect us most. Case in point: me in Cambridge, hoping to become the next Barack Obama, not aware that Obama's administration was joining other Western powers in mutilating an African country, grabbing its resources, and cutting off its plans to empower the continent. Yeah, I was fully clueless back then. But if someone had helped me connect these dots, I'd have understood that this was nothing new.

A Toxic Relationship

For six hundred years, Europe and America have consistently demonstrated their disregard for non-White life. Over the last sixty years in particular, Western powers have entangled African nations in a matrix of debt and economic dependency, ensured by organisations like the International Monetary Fund (IMF) and the World Bank. These two represent the West's stranglehold on the global economy, which in many ways is a more brutal force than physical warfare. The IMF spent the final decades of the twentieth century putting African and Caribbean countries on a devastating course of 'structural adjustment' – pretending to help them grow by forcing their governments to cut spending, sell national assets and allow foreign capitalists to do whatever they want in their economies.

Jamaica provided an early example of this in the 1970s, when socialist leader Michael Manley ran the country into debt by investing heavily in social programmes for the poor. His timing couldn't have been worse: oil prices had shot up and commodity prices (which the country relied on) were crashing. Plus, America was pursuing several strategies to weaken the country, out of concern for Manley's friendship with the communist leader of nearby Cuba, Fidel Castro. When Jamaica was financially on the ropes, in came the IMF with a loan that required the 'structural adjustment' of the country's economy. Reverend Renaldo McKenzie details the havoc this wreaked on the lives of Jamaicans in his 2021 book, *Neoliberalism, Globalization, Income Inequality, Poverty and Resistance*.[17] Over the next few decades, this became the story of most nations in the global South.

The relationship between Afro-descended peoples and the West is a toxic one. This is why, for as long as I can remember, in our corner of Black Britain no one trusted the government, the police or the media. In fact, now that I think about it, the North West London Jamaican community exposed me to Black critical thought at a young age; it was a core part of the supplementary education once provided for the community's children by their elders, as well as the Rastafari culture surrounding us all. But, as explained earlier, being a radical is hard, and being a liberal is easy. Many of us want a fairer world

– just not at the cost of our personal comfort and security. We work for whoever will pay us the most, and that's rarely a grassroots pro-Black organisation. We rely on global supply chains that make everything available to us in our nearest supermarkets, and we enjoy perks of Western rule like getting paid in strong currencies and living on the safer side of almost any war. These are the things that keep us locked in this toxic relationship. But regardless, as Black radicalism reminds us, we'll never earn enough Western money, win enough Western votes or control enough Western industry to reset this relationship peacefully. This is what the liberal in me wasn't ready to face at the start of my Cambridge journey.

Borders

For even the most optimistic Black liberal, however, Western migration policies offer a sobering reminder of how one-sided this relationship is. Europe enlists African governments to stem the flow of Africans to its shores – a flow that is driven by poverty resulting from the same Western-induced economic dependency I described not long ago. 'We want your land and your labour – not your people,' seems to be the message. In the 2000s, the Seahorse Network 'trained' Africans and allowed EU ships in waters around Cape Verde, Senegal, Morocco and Mauritania to catch migrants attempting to reach Europe, reducing the number of intercepted Africans from 31,000 in 2006 to 332 in 2013. The EU's West Sahel Project did the same in 2015, strengthening surveillance in the area. These militarised strategies of border control were described by the Pan-African Network in Defense of Migrants' Rights as 'hunting policies for migrants that grow everywhere on the African continent with the support of the European institutions under the guise of the fight against irregular migration'. And yeah, money also played a part. African leaders are often bribed with aid tied to migration control, like when the EU effectively paid Sudan's former leader Omar al-Bashir over €150 million to keep those Africans in Africa. Over the past few years, the UK government has tried to set up a similar arrangement with Rwandan leader Paul Kagame – sending over asylum seekers rejected by the UK who aren't even from Rwanda. It's even more twisted that the ruling Conservative Party has used non-White people like former UK Home Secretaries Priti Patel and Suella Braverman to be the face of these racist policies. Despite being forced to admit that she couldn't identify a single legal route available to migrants, Braverman continued to demonise and dehumanise asylum seekers at every opportunity.[18] Still, in my opinion, nowhere has the keep-Africans-in-Africa money been better spent for Europe and more devastatingly for Africans than in Libya.

In the late 2000s, when Gaddafi began openly campaigning for a single African currency backed by gold, the clock started ticking for Libya's leader and the country's era of stability. There really is no doubt that his proposal would have shifted the global power balance in Africa's favour. Can you imagine what would happen if all the Congolese minerals in our devices, all the Nigerian oil in our engines, and all the Ghanaian cocoa in our cups *had* to be paid using that single African currency?

A Cambridge Man

I'm serious when I say your understanding of Gaddafi's currency project says a lot about your understanding of the world. You can't assess our political reality without studying the economic logic of Western power, and the resistance strategies it has spawned across the world. Yet, by design, Western society props up 'intellectuals' who have never given this any thought. Their worldview is rooted in a version of history in which the good guys won. This makes it impossible for these 'intellectuals' to imagine that a huge proportion of the world is deeply unhappy with the way things are.

Previously, I told you how Samira and Dee, two Black women I met at this party, were sharing their feelings of alienation from the Black British working-class struggle, before Dee's White husband, Will, took the conversation in a different direction. I explained in the Introduction how I ended up pushing back against his approach because a lot of what he said was intellectually clumsy, and he didn't bother listening before talking. Will didn't like that and told me I was treating him unfairly because he was White, so I put myself in his shoes. I pictured a different group of people having a conversation about something that I, like Will, had opinions on, and a connection to via my wife, but no direct experience of. I channelled Will's overconfidence, knowing I should be heard despite my lack of original research or first-hand insight. In my mind's eye, I saw Sandra talking with some women she'd just met about their experience of womanhood in the world of work. Then I pictured myself 'innocently' telling them that things are better for women than they might realise. Once I had the scenario in my head, I broke it down to Will like this: 'Bro, if I entered a conversation between three women about things they go through as women, I would be in listening mode. No matter how strongly I felt about what they might be saying, as a man I wouldn't be able to speak to their experience. My point to you is about this awareness. As a White person, you're entitled to your opinion, but you should be mindful of these dynamics in conversations about race with Black people.' He still didn't get it.

Will got more and more agitated as the conversation progressed. He took what I said as an attack on his right to have an opinion, centring his emotions in a conversation that was initially about the Black experience. It drove him crazy that I had the audacity to suggest his Whiteness meant he should tread more carefully. I had seen this outrage countless times, and was well aware that many White people hate nothing more than being seen as White people. It took me years to understand this, but that reaction comes from a lifelong privilege of not having to think seriously about race. Someone with this privilege is less likely to understand that darker populations have been excluded from the power network of White supremacy at every meaningful level. This network was developed by the most influential European institutions of all time – from religious institutions like the Catholic church to legal institutions like property law and, of course, educational institutions like the University of Cambridge. Through universities especially, ideas about Whiteness were developed 'scientifically', and presented as common sense to the White masses. But this history isn't taught on a compulsory basis, so White people are often left unaware of how deeply racist their societies are. That lack of awareness makes it upsetting for someone like Will to be confronted by someone like me, who seems to have judged Whiteness before giving every White individual a blank slate to define it for me. Not everyone has time for that BS. Being woken up by your alarm is one of the most stressful moments of your day, but for the sake of getting things done, you get out of bed.

I take full responsibility for allowing the conversation to drag on as long as it did. And, even though I felt awkward about pressuring Dee's man in front of her, I couldn't leave any room for him to gaslight her on the way home. It's not that I was Dee's protector; more that, since she hadn't disagreed with me, and was even affirming my points here and there, I got the impression they argued about this a lot. Dee basically confirmed that when she said, 'Honestly, I tell him this all the time.' Will didn't even look embarrassed when she said it. If anything, he seemed excited at the opportunity to perform his routine in front of a new Black audience. What Dee said to her husband next shocked me even more, although it really shouldn't have: 'All you Cambridge types are so sure of yourselves.' It was a joke, but it also felt like a lifeline to her husband – a tactful way of restoring his image in an uncomfortable situation. Will's face broke into a smile immediately. I could see from his lack of acknowledgement that he didn't even recognise how Dee had just helped him out.

'Oh yeah, you're a *Cambridge* man!' he said, like he was proud to recognise something in me that reminded him of himself. I've never felt so embarrassed to be called that. Not because of anything I or the university did, just for the fact that Will reflected us both. *This* guy went to Cambridge. What does that say about me, and the institution that incubated me for three years?

By this point, the four of us had been talking for what felt like forty minutes, and like I said, Will just sounded more whiny and oblivious as he went on. Not one part of him felt any shame at his arrogance backfiring in front of his wife, who had apparently tried to advise him about it for years. This situation made me see Will's Whiteness as a passport so powerful that he never felt the need for a visa. He didn't think he needed permission to go where he wanted, and he didn't care what wrong turns he made on his way there. I realised that this mentality meant the guy rarely felt out of place – even when his own wife and a complete stranger were looking at him like he was crazy. He couldn't recognise when he was out of his depth because he was used to defining 'deep' for himself. To a man like this, if the woman he loved, respected and trusted enough to start a family with happened to believe that her Blackness gave her insights that his Whiteness withheld from him, then she was making a shallow point. That's a long way of saying *this Cambridge man thought he was deep*.

The Cambridge Effect

If Cambridge offered a degree in Black Studies, I would have taken it. The fact that this option wasn't available suggested to me that the university didn't see Blackness as a viable academic field – a view that pervades Western academia to this day. At the time, I clung to Politics and Sociology as subjects that I'd eventually use to navigate my way through the Black struggle. My plan was to learn methods of interpreting the world that would help me break out of the hopelessness I'd been resisting since childhood. But who knows? Maybe it's best that the university didn't intervene in my study of Black life. Maybe a Cambridge course in Blackness would have confused things for me and left me with the same misplaced confidence I perceived in Will.

When I think back to the importance of Gaddafi's overthrow, which took place during my first year, and the fact that not a single lecturer made any reference to it at the time, I'm actually glad that I got into Black Studies independently. Don't get me wrong, I'd still pick a well-designed Africana degree over the Eurocentric one I ended up with, but at least I didn't waste years having the Black experience explained to me by an institution so closely linked to Britain's imperial core.

10

Momentum

During that first year of Cambridge, I started performing poetry that I thought was deep, when in reality I hadn't scratched the surface of what my life's work would need to address. My early poems were a combination of stories from the neighbourhood and venting sessions about the neighbourhood. To be fair, this is what most Rap consists of. My performance at *Culture Fest* went down great, and the following month my college's student union (KCSU) held elections for a new council to represent the student voice. I'm not sure what drew me to the role of Chairman. Maybe it was my guy from school, Kalil, being President of the ACS. Maybe it was the fear of one day feeling like I didn't make the most of my time at King's. Either way, it presented a challenge that appealed to me. I told a few friends, made a Facebook page and started campaigning between lectures. Competition came from a handful of other students, which I liked – it proved that the position meant something. Within a week, we would all have to go head-to-head in a showdown at the student bar where all the candidates gave a speech aimed at winning votes. This was called the 'hustings'. Cambridge was full of words that everyone seemed to know apart from me. I didn't care though – I had a plan: I was going to make my whole speech rhyme.

When I told Kalil about the plan to rhyme my way through a KCSU campaign, even *he* couldn't take it. 'Don't,' he said, thinking it would be too much too soon. He couldn't talk me out of it, but when the day of the hustings came, I wasn't so sure. I was actually annoyed at myself because I hadn't memorised the speech. Looking back now, I think I held myself to an impossible standard, expecting to write a campaign speech in rhyme and memorise it in a week. This was harder than memorising a normal verse because I didn't have an instrumental and, for once, the rhymes weren't about me. On the evening of the hustings, I sat in the student bar holding two sheets of A4 paper, cramming the words I was about to deliver, while each candidate addressed the hundred or so students who showed up. I remember feeling good about how bland most of their speeches were but thrown by how seriously everyone was taking themselves. Maybe Kalil was right. Was I about to box myself in as the token Black guy? I shrugged, thinking, *It is what it is.* The ability to rhyme made me smarter, not dumber.

When my turn finally came, I stood up, grabbed the microphone and surprisingly delivered the majority of my words without looking at the paper. I gave the audience no warning that it would be a poetry performance, so they were expecting another normal speech. When I saw faces light up as they caught on to the rhyme scheme, I relaxed. This was going to work. I won the election by a landslide, and quickly settled into my new role as KCSU Chairman. I didn't know it at the time, but this would be my last moment of real optimism about my place in King's.

The Language

It didn't take long for the loneliness to set in. My course was interesting, and the people were friendly, but socially it didn't click for me. As expected, the workload was intense; we had to write four essays a week and defend them the following week to a group made up of one expert and a few other students. These weekly meetings were called supervisions, and they were part of what made Cambridge so challenging, academically. The supervisor would usually be a heavyweight in their field – someone who wrote the main book on the reading list. The other students were ambitious, gifted young people – mainly women on my course. I rarely finished all my essays, so would often roll up to supervisions and wing it. I wanted to be a model student, like Kalil and my course-mate Yuho, but I read slowly and wrote even slower. This made it hard for me to concentrate, both in lectures and in the library. During the first twenty minutes of a lecture, I'd be on point, writing detailed notes and thinking deeply about what the lecturer was saying. Then I'd get bored and need to move around or talk.

Now that I'm a professional writer, I understand that sitting in a big hall watching one person lecture in a non-creative way isn't intellectually engaging for me. But back then, I just felt bad for not being like everyone else. Sometimes after a lecture, I'd spend the whole day in the library, trying to read a book and write an essay on it. But most of what I wanted to know was hidden in complicated, dry language that killed my curiosity. I was studying things I cared about in an environment I admired, but trying to actually get to the knowledge was a nightmare. Years later, when I finally realised how badly this academic language alienated me from a lot of powerful ideas, I started recognising the same alienation across the Black diaspora. Dry language that most modern Brits don't even use is super-demotivating for any young person, but Black students have a particularly strenuous relationship with English in general.

Think about all the segregation that has been normalised in Europe over the past few centuries. African versions of

European languages grew up under these conditions – both on the continent and in the diaspora. Sometimes when I'm listening to the Francophone lyrics of Congolese music, I can hear the same Bantu twang of Ugandan languages. And even though I don't understand French, when I hear West Africans speak it, their accents sound like Nigerian English to me. These linguistic connections might explain why wherever we settle in the world, Black people remix language in ways that are consistent between communities far apart. Experts on this trend can probably trace it through ancient African cultures, but I mainly see it in West African and Afro-Caribbean dialects. Growing up in the diaspora, I was exposed to both, so I hear similarities between them despite their people being torn apart centuries ago. For example, in Nigerian pidgin, 'pikin' means 'child', similar to the Caribbean word 'pickney'; the Igbo term 'únù' means 'you all', as it does in Jamaican patois; and in both regions, the word 'dey/deh' is used similarly too. Underlying parallels like these are rich and beautiful, but they represent only one side of the coin. On the other side, there's the fact that European languages in African life represent violence. These were the languages used to negotiate the sale of Africans into slavery. They were imposed on Africans and used to spread things that suffocated African ways of life, like Christianity and capitalism. This has resulted in a relationship of dominance, whereby Afro-descended peoples are forced to comply with European practices, including language. It's a dynamic of trauma.

So, unique African styles of speech and the unhappy entry of European languages into Black life both underpin the strenuous relationship Black people often have with English. For this reason, we can't help but remix the language, because even when we speak it 'properly' as individuals, we still live in unofficially segregated communities en masse. As a result, diaspora English develops differently to mainstream English. In diasporic communities, the mixing of different Black cultures creates a new accent out of the average of our ancestors' accents. I'm a product of this process; although I learned formal English, my siblings and I grew up using the Jamaican English of Black London and, inevitably, the Ugandan English of our parents. Half the time, I didn't even recognise the effects of these influences, since we picked them up informally. But let me be clear: I don't mean to imply that Black vernacular English is inferior to formal English, or that Black people speak differently because they can't speak 'properly'. Our vernacular dialect is my favourite form of English, but here's the best way I can put it: *Black performance of White language is similar to White performance of Black music; we can do it, but we can't help doing it 'our' way.*

Voices

What did this mean for my studies? The voice I used to read in was different from the voice I used to speak in. To make life easier, I've always tried to merge the two, which isn't straightforward; a regular phrase in one part of my life may not translate in another. And why is that significant? Because this disconnect represents the experience a lot of Black people have with Western education in general – especially in language-based subjects. Being assessed by Western institutions on your ability to reproduce Western ideas using Western language feels, for many of us, like trying to look natural in someone else's clothes. It's one of the ways in which, as some of our parents told us, we have to work twice as hard to do half as well. A White student immersed in mainstream English, from their home life to their social life, experiences less friction when reading texts that sound closer to *their* own internal voice than mine. Of course, that doesn't mean every White person enjoys reading Sociology more than me, or finds it easier than I do, but it is a serious factor in educational outcomes. My struggle to keep up with the reading, combined with my newfound isolation, led to a daily pattern of *lecture-library-dorm room*. Without a social scene that had the music, food and conversations I missed so badly, I became a loner. And this is when I discovered that loneliness and poetry go hand in hand.

By the age of nineteen, writing verses had grown into a habit. It was a pastime born out of my earlier Grime years; a combination of work and play that always felt like opening a window and letting in some fresh air. Anytime I was on my own with a lot on my mind, the easiest thing to do was write a rhyme. Not only was it fun; it eased the tension in my body, and put me in a calm, reflective state. For some reason, nothing fuelled this habit like reading Sociology. I would make it halfway through a chapter of some old theory book, get hung up on a particular point the author made, and drift off into my own writing. This was the part where the study of society changed me as an artist. Reading about why we live the way we do made me want to invite more people to the conversation. Instead of trying to translate the ideas of different theorists, I wrote my own observations without shying away from social analysis. Since most of my real-world experience came from where I grew up, my verses usually reflected the anxieties of Black urban youth, relating directly to poverty, crime and family-related trauma. The writing would always happen at the desk in my dorm room, before progressing to a performance direct to camera, recorded in that same spot. I still remember the earliest poems from this period, like ‘Lemonade’. Looking back on the second stanza of that poem, I can see that I was starting to write about overlapping issues in a joined-up way:

She was the sket who stayed out with these fellas.
It took a paedophile to breed the child
The seed was wild and she’s just down on her knees
Praying he don’t learn how to be a menace . . .
Tryna make lemonade out of these lemons.
And if you ask her why she’ll say ‘That lemon’s mine
And it’s sour but it never was a clementine.’
See, the fact that life is sweet for <u>them</u> is fine but
This world was designed with them in mind.

Increasingly, I honed my voice on the journey to amplify the voices of others. By articulating the experiences of those around me, I discovered my role as a narrator of Black life.

African Caribbean Societies to the Rescue

When the Cambridge African Caribbean Society (ACS) shared with me an invitation from Nottingham to perform at a collaborative showcase with ACSs from other universities, I jumped at the opportunity. This was near the end of my first term, by which point I was starving for anything Black, and itching to get back on stage. Students from the universities of Nottingham and Nottingham Trent ran an annual event called *Jazz, Funk and Soul*, showcasing talent from African Caribbean Societies across the country. I heard someone say there would be fifteen different unis present. Some of the organisers had attended *Culture Fest* and decided that I’d be a good fit. To this day, I'm grateful for the forward-thinking network these young leaders formed among themselves. Cambridge ACS was arranging a coach to take a group of us up there for the evening and back; all I had to do was perform for about five minutes. At the time, my twentieth birthday was on the horizon. I was broke and overworked, frustrated by my nightly cycle of dreaming I was back in Uganda and waking up to cold-ass Cambridge. But still, every morning I rose with a little more knowledge than the day before. My twenty minutes of attention at the start of lectures made a difference to my perspective, and I benefited from just trying to keep up. One side-effect was the acceleration of my new creative drive: poetry. After delivering an election campaign speech in poetic form, I realised that everything was more interesting when it rhymed. This made me write more and more, channelling my education and my experiences into what I now understood as 'Spoken Word'. So, by the time *Jazz, Funk and Soul* came around, I was a lot readier than I had been for *Culture Fest* a few months before.

In early January, the big day arrived. I never found out how many universities were in the audience, but it was clearly a lot. The hall was massive – maybe the biggest I had ever performed in up to that date, and as soon as we got off the coach from Cambridge, I felt those familiar nerves. *Jazz, Funk and Soul* was my introduction to a whole new facet of the Black community: young, mainly Nigerian, mainly British-born, mainly Christian university students. This wasn't the only demographic, but it was a very vocal majority. I had never really grown up with Nigerians, apart from Damini, the school friend I introduced you to earlier. Generally, my social life was dominated by Caribbeans and, later, Ugandans. Here, at *Jazz, Funk and Soul*, I stepped into another world. Everyone was dressed to kill, and no matter how cool we acted, most of us had never been part of anything like this before: a whole university link-up – for us, by us. There were good vibes in the air, like we were all proud to be there and proud to see each other there too. It would take years for me to learn that the wave of African migration to Britain in the 1980s, following the frustrations of decolonisation on the continent, led to a sudden influx of Africans in Britain who experienced the country differently to their Afro-Caribbean counterparts of the previous few decades. These new African immigrants benefited from hard-won victories against institutional racism fought by generations of British Caribbeans. And now, this link-up opened my eyes to the fact our generation had come of age. This was my story, as much as theirs; I was also a child of immigrants who left Africa after Independence didn't work out. I was also representing the hard work and sacrifice of Africans and Afro-Caribbeans before me. I felt honoured to carry such a responsibility.

That night, I took to the stage and performed a poem called 'Gyalist in Wonderland', a funny story about the dangers of promiscuity. The audience loved it. They held their breath throughout, only breaking the silence to gasp and laugh at all the right moments, begging for an encore when I was finished. The energy in the hall was electric; I knew I was in their minds because I was telling a story they recognised in a way they'd never heard before. This time, I had taken the calculated risk of performing without music, and it paid off. Somehow, after years of trying to make it in Grime and almost giving up on Rap, I had found a new creative direction using my voice alone. If this reaction had come from a song that I'd performed with music produced by someone else, it would be impossible to tell how much the audience identified with my thoughts.

After *Jazz, Funk and Soul*, demand for my live performances went through the roof, taking me all over the country to perform for other ACSs that were there that night, and eventually to those they had spread the word to. I had never experienced anything like it. When I met an older poet called Suli Breaks at a show for Aston University's ACS, he advised me to put my material on YouTube. It's crazy to think that in 2011 this didn't occur to me. Suli's advice turned out to be crucial in boosting the demand for my work, as thousands of people gradually flocked around this new experiment online. Thanks, Suli.

The next big milestone came at an event called *Vocals & Verses*, where a young, predominantly West African crowd was so moved by my words that they interrupted me with applause less than one minute in, and demanded I start again from the top. In Jamaican sound-system culture, this is called a 'wheel-up', or 'pull-up' or 'reload' – a climax in a musical event, when a crowd's reaction to a song causes the DJ to restart it. The term travelled over to Britain via the Caribbean community and became a big part of Grime culture. Up to that point, a poet getting a wheel-up was unheard of. In fact, during my four years as an MC, this had never happened to me outside of my peer group. It was surreal for my first real pull-up to come from a room full of strangers, not at a hyper Grime set, but at a calm poetry performance with pretty girls and clean-cut guys. It was clear that in six months of Spoken Word, I'd generated more of a buzz than I did in four years of Grime. There was no turning back from here.

11

From Community to Mainstream

I Signed a Record Deal

Two life-changing things happened for me in the summer of 2013: I graduated from Cambridge and I signed a record deal. When Universal Music's Island Records heard about me, they followed the hype. Darcus Beese, the most senior Black man in the British music industry, made an impressive pitch to me on behalf of Island, which he was the President of. Darcus explained that he shared my passion for the Black community, as the son of two former members of the British Black Panther Party: Darcus Howe and Barbara Beese. I can't lie, I was impressed with his parents. Both of them were arrested in 1970 as part of the Mangrove Nine, a group of Black activists charged with inciting a riot during a protest against the police harassment of a Caribbean restaurant in West London called The Mangrove. The subsequent trial found them all innocent of the most serious charge (inciting a riot), and marked the first time a British court acknowledged racism in the police force. Darcus Sr went on to become a prominent figure in Black British politics, fighting those battles I mentioned earlier – the ones Caribbeans fought before Africans arrived in big numbers over here. Fast-forward forty years, and there I was, signing a record contract with Darcus Jr, who can be seen as a kid in photos of the protests his parents frequented. Darcus knew his background mattered to me. He'd recently attended my sold-out show, *Malik*, which was all about Malcolm X. In fact, it was right after that show that Darcus walked up to me backstage and told me he would make sure the world heard my voice. To his credit, he was the only label head who showed any personal connection to my work, which was important at the time, given that Island Records had entered a bidding war with competitors Virgin and Atlantic, both of which had passionate A&Rs trying to sign me too.

I was wary of the music industry. During that final year of Cambridge, I took a paper called 'Media, Culture and Society', in which I learned about the shrinking ownership of mass media, i.e. most mainstream music being owned by those three powerful companies I mentioned earlier. I had read about the effect this had on the cultural landscape, and how the profit motive of these companies favoured standardised production techniques, leading to less innovation in music. Not only had I read it, I'd seen it in the demise of Grime a few years earlier, as leading artists from our (then underground) scene signed to major labels and released bland, watered-down tracks that hurt their credibility but made the record companies happy. I knew the same could happen to me, and I signed the deal anyway. My reasoning was that I'd already taken poetry surprisingly far, but it still wasn't mainstream enough to capture a nationwide audience.

To be clear, I had been on a roll up to that point. In under two years, I'd gone from my first poetry performance to headline shows and TV appearances. A diverse range of listeners showed me that there was a market for my style of Spoken Word. By the time I signed this record deal, my audience had expanded beyond the Black British student network to include the Rap scene, middle-class liberals in the South, working-class communities in the North and even a significant corporate following. I wrote whatever I felt, and the demand kept growing. Eventually, I started reintroducing music into my work, and this was when the record labels took notice.

The first experiment came from the mind of my friend, fellow British Ugandan Rashid Kasirye, founder of the online music platform, Link Up TV. I was chilling at Rashid's place during my last year of school when he first shared the idea of Link Up TV with me. Back then I was an MC, so he offered to record me performing one of my verses for this new channel. In the short time since then, Link Up TV had blown up, becoming a leading provider of music-related content from the emerging Road Rap scene. Not for the first time, Rashid established himself as a legend in the hood. Prior to this he was a Grime producer called Ice Cold, whose instrumentals went viral throughout North West London. The guy was a genuine hustler who kept his ear to the streets, and he always used his influence to support me. Towards the end of 2011, only a year into my poetry career, Rashid booked me to perform at a live show for Link Up TV. This being at the height of the Road Rap era, the venue was full of community rappers, who seemed like the event was their only break from street activity that week. I got on stage and for the third or fourth time that year, my words sparked such a burst of energy that I got a wheel-up: the audience shouted their approval and demanded that I start again, so they could properly take in my thoughts. I added that night to the growing list of favours Rashid had already done me.

In my former life as a struggling MC, Rashid advised me to take my mixtape to the Harlesden radio station Bang FM (now Beat FM). There I met two young women called Lynnike and Sefa, DJs for the station who were passionate about local talent. They both took to me instantly, and saw the potential in my amateur mixtape, way before I even had the notion of poetry. In this sense, Rashid, Lynnike and Sefa were just like countless other community figures who nurtured young talent. In the years before my fame, I met dozens of producers, DJs, youth workers and impresarios who constantly affirmed my dreams with positive feedback about how unique and talented I was, at a time when my abilities were raw and easy to dismiss. I wish there were secure jobs available for everyone doing this work because it goes a long way in drawing out the best of our young people. Later on, in my first year of poetry, Lynnike and Sefa introduced me to Lioness, a widely respected female rapper from South London. Lioness liked what I was doing and invited me to perform at the launch of her EP, *Roarness*, in September 2011. Her audience was mainly street rappers from South London, so the last thing they expected was a poet from Cambridge, as I was known then. Still, they continued the trend of hanging onto my every word, and exploding with emotion as I vented my frustrations onstage. In the audience was a film director called Rob Ryan, who later pushed me to write a poem about London in the wake of the 2011 riots, and ahead of the 2012 London Olympics. I called it 'My City', and we shot a gritty video for it. Rob was instrumental in getting me back in front of the camera, which I had been avoiding for reasons I can't remember. 'My City' went on to generate a surge of interest, culminating in a series of poems for Channel 4's *Random Acts* TV show. I was blown away when Channel 4 reported that these poems received the highest viewer count across TV for their respective time slot. As if that wasn't crazy enough, the BBC then asked me to write and perform a poem promoting their big music festival, the Radio 1 Hackney Weekender – headlined that year by Jay-Z and Kanye West. This poem would be broadcast across the country in primetime

TV slots, furthering the process of introducing me to a mainstream audience. Studying Sociology at Cambridge while building a cross-sectional following from the underground Rap scene to mainstream TV was like living all my teenage dreams at once. And it was all happening so quickly.

Months later, in the spring of 2012, halfway through my university course, Rashid called me with an idea. He suggested that I team up with a talented piano player from his old school, who I had met in his flat back in the day. The guy's name was Emmanuel Stanleys. Like us, Emmanuel was the son of African immigrants, and he grew up in Harlesden. He played piano in church and had developed that musical intuition that so many church musicians have. Rashid's idea was for Emmanuel to play while I performed, which he would film and share on the Link Up TV YouTube channel. It was a smart, collaborative way of diversifying his platform and promoting his friends. Made sense to me. I wanted Emmanuel to play something recognisable to the Rap audience and, after experiencing so much success without music, I was cautious about anything that would clash with my voice. 'Dead Presidents', by Jay-Z, seemed like a good choice. It had a classic piano loop sampled from 'A Garden of Peace' by Lonnie Liston-Smith, which I figured would be familiar to most Rap listeners my age. The associations attached to the music were important because they sent a message about where I was positioning myself culturally.

For some weeks, I listened to 'Dead Presidents' over and over, and eventually wrote a poem reflecting on the changing role of my generation within our community. We were growing up, becoming the guys that influenced the choices of kids around us. The poem, which I called 'The Olders', was a plea to my peers caught up in street life, imploring them to leave the next generation out of it. As planned, Emmanuel and I recorded a performance of it at the Link Up TV studios in Park Royal, near where we all grew up. Even though I was nervous, Emmanuel played perfectly, gliding over the keys like it was just another Sunday service. Rashid filmed the performance and, when he uploaded it to YouTube, the reaction was instant. An outpouring of appreciation from listeners across the internet confirmed that this experiment had done its job. The poem received 9,000 views in its first twenty-four hours, which climbed to 30,000 the next day. Sure, this isn't ground-breaking by today's standards, but back then it was phenomenal. We recorded three more poems for Link Up TV over the next couple of months, and that collection has gone down as a turning point in my career, when I not only reached a mass audience of UK Rap fans, but also established myself as a commentator on street culture.

Language as a Tool

When I look back on this period of my life, placing social analysis at the core of my art is the creative breakthrough that I'm most thankful for. From writing rhymes in between lectures to signing a record deal within two years, I underwent a creative rebirth based on new ways of experiencing language. I'm one hundred per cent sure that the complexity of my course material at Cambridge influenced me to push myself lyrically. If I could decode the language of books on developmental psychology and comparative studies of kinship, then surely I could represent our community in a new way. Even though, at this stage, I didn't have a detailed plan of what to write or why, I felt I had found something that would lead me in the right direction. All the validation I needed came from the community that taught me how to rhyme in the first place; from local radio to the Link Up TV audience, excitement around my new approach to lyricism carried me from obscurity to the mainstream. And eventually, by signing a deal with Island Records, I hoped to signal to my fellow artists that there were ways of using language that could allow us to further our careers without falling into popular, but damaging, portrayals of the Black experience. I guess I was partly right.

PART III

The Long Run

12

A Racial Hierarchy

My early success in poetry gave me confidence. I felt like I had come up with my own thing and it touched the hearts of people I'd never met. Even though I was in Cambridge during this time, my friends back home let me know my words were being heard – and so did the rest of the community. Up to this point, that was as far as my dreams could reach – being *heard*. I kind of knew this wasn't the be-all and end-all, but being heard on a national scale was so rare for anyone from our area that it seemed like a gigantic achievement. Still, after they've heard you, life goes on. The situation that moved you to speak up either continues as it was, unbothered by your voice, or it changes. My poetry was motivated by the need to document the hardships around me, and I was stressed out at the thought of those hardships continuing unchanged while my poems saw success from talking about them. That would be like making a reality TV show about a friend's terminal illness for my own personal gain. I had to figure out how this poetry could be used to ensure that the situation it came from would be improved by its success.

I didn't realise it at the time, but I had just done eighteen years in an education system that limited my understanding of this problem. If you went through the same system as me, you could come out of it believing racial inequality wasn't *important* enough to study. In fact, at the time of writing, Britain's Conservative government doesn't even believe structural racism exists in this country. So, imagine me trying to break down the challenges of my predominantly Black community through poetry, to a country that proudly thinks of itself as 'colour-blind'. This at a time when a lot of White people were insisting 'It's not about race anymore – the real struggle is class!' My Cambridge degree didn't give me the wisdom, experience or authority to shut these arguments down. In fact, nothing I'd ever studied in school actually gave me the words to address what had been staring me in the face the whole time: my daily journey from the Black inner city to the White suburbs, in the name of education; the almost all-White teaching staff at my school, contrasting with the all-Black cleaning staff; the clear differences in wealth and life experiences across my year group – differences that had an ethnic pattern. All of this pointed to a racial hierarchy.

Europe and Africa – a Brief History

Around six hundred years ago, Europe was in bad shape. The Plague had wiped out between 30 and 60 per cent of its population, leading to mass shortages of labour. On top of that, European trade was hit by a balance-of-payments crisis, triggered by supplies of both European silver and African gold drying up. The continent wasn't producing much that could compete with the luxury fabrics and spices of the East, leaving it heavily dependent on gold from Sudan (supplied by itinerant traders). For this reason, when leadership struggles in the dominant Mali Empire led to the decline of gold production towards the late 1300s, Europe experienced a shortage of money. In his book *Born in Blackness*, the Pulitzer-nominated journalist Howard French describes it like this:

> Gold coinage in England cratered in this era, from an annual average of £56,064 during the 1360s to a yearly average of £4,715 in the decade from 1401 to 1410. This led to a severe contraction in liquidity and the reversion with a vengeance to a more primitive economic system based on barter.[19]

In response to this crisis, the Portuguese started looking for the source of African gold, with hopes of controlling the trade themselves. They were motivated by the legend of Mansa Musa, who had led the Mali Empire during its heyday just decades prior. Rap music is full of references to this king, whose vast wealth was made legendary by an epic trip to Cairo, during which he gave out so much gold that the price of the metal plummeted for years. Mansa Musa is still recorded as the richest man that ever lived. The Portuguese desire to tap into that wealth led them to capture Ceuta, a small city on the edge of modern-day Morocco, in 1415. This didn't end up being the big break they were hoping for, since Ceuta was neither rich nor crucial to the gold trade. Still, the Portuguese decided to keep control of the city, leading to the first case of European colonisation in Africa.

It's crazy that this story never came up in school, considering it birthed the world we live in today. In search of gold, the Portuguese grabbed small territories in the Mediterranean Sea that provided stepping stones to mainland Africa, like the tiny island of Madeira. Here they enslaved the locals and employed indentured labourers (outcasts of Portuguese society) to create the earliest attempt at a sugar colony – another precursor of the world to come. The success of this sugar prompted the Portuguese to import enslaved people from nearby islands but, as demand soared, so did the need for more land and more forced labour. You see where I'm going with this. Portugal's activities off the West African coast became the primary driver of wealth, not just for them, but for the whole neighbourhood of Western Europe.

I was never really taught the history of slavery. It was treated like a bad dream: no one seemed to remember how it started, the details were always hazy and most of the focus went on how it ended. The message I got from school (and society in general) was that today's world doesn't have anything to do with the slave trade. But that couldn't be further from the truth. When they finally made contact with African states, the Portuguese found complex societies that would be much harder to dominate than Ceuta and Madeira. In fact, they were often in awe, unable to overwhelm the Africans militarily, and therefore compelled to build diplomatic links based on trade – as they did with the kingdoms of Akan, Benin and Kongo. These mutually respectful relations lasted for centuries, but eventually they gave way to the ever-expanding European appetite for African slaves. Slavery was more lucrative than gold, because slaves were people that could dig up gold, and produce more people to dig up more gold. In fact, slaves could be forced to dig, plant, harvest, build or do *anything*, and if the work killed them, they could just be replaced. This was a hard drug. Many African leaders sold other Africans into slavery (and, in a way, many still do) but their options have always been dictated by the European exploitation of African politics, aimed at securing African workers who could be used to build European industries and societies that Africans themselves would be locked out of.

In her 2021 book, *Border & Rule*, seasoned activist Harsha Walia explains that while African land is continuously smothered by European capital, 'highly subsidised European agribusinesses are dumping food into African markets and further displacing farmers. Tomato, grains, dairy products and coffee are flooding African markets. Meanwhile, oil, copper, cobalt, diamonds, uranium, zinc, iron, bauxite, coal, coltan and gold are dug up and exported for corporate profit.'[20] To show how this manufacturing of poverty drives irregular migration, Walia provides the following example:

> Europe's fishing agreement with Mauritania gives over one hundred EU vessels access to fishing waters off the coast of Mauritania, resulting in the devastation of local livelihoods. Yet, if impoverished fishers attempt to migrate, they get apprehended by an EU surveillance vessel.

This is the racial hierarchy: the guardians of Western wealth maintain a balancing act of inequality to secure their privilege at the expense of everyone else. This balancing act is an art that they have been perfecting since the 1400s.

The Racist Division of Labour

By the early 1500s, Portugal and Spain had invaded the Americas, later joined by their neighbours Holland, Britain and France. Portugal took the pattern from its earliest colonies in and around Africa and exported it to Brazil. This meant organising large groups of enslaved Africans across big plantations, where they would work on different parts of a massive operation. Usually the operation involved producing something that the Portuguese could profit from in at least three ways: shipping it, selling it or using it to make something else. This made Portugal and Spain very rich in a short space of time, and others saw similar growth when they followed suit, triggering a wave of colonisation. As the first case of a few

Europeans running a whole region mainly populated by darker peoples, colonial projects of the 1400s had taught the Portuguese this much: colonisation could be made to pay for itself; plantation work would kill a lot of slaves, so it was necessary to keep a constant supply of them coming; dark skin made it easier for a White person to identify a slave, minimising the risk of them slipping away; and it was best to keep slaves divided by ensuring their inability to communicate.

It doesn't take a genius to see how this racist violence underpinned the empires that European powers grew into over the following centuries. When I finally started reading about slavery as an adult, memories of History lessons from school came back to me, reminding me how hard Britain worked to highlight every aspect of its backstory other than the African flesh that made the country so rich. I remembered the long essay I wrote about the Battle of Hastings in 1066 (Year 7); I remembered being taught that Henry VIII broke away from the Catholic church (Year 8); I even remembered some of his wives' names. Next, I remembered studying the 1800s – a lot. Steam power, the Corn Laws, the creation of the police force, Queen Victoria wearing black because her man died, then straight into the 1900s with the World Wars. No mention of the ongoing slavery that endured across the British Empire during this period for decades after the abolition of the slave trade in 1807. This was the only national history we learned about from Year 9 through to the end of my school years. It wasn't until later I noticed we completely skipped the 1700s – the century when slave labour made Britain a superpower. You would think the country didn't know Black people existed before the Civil Rights Movement. In reality, since the 1600s Britain had been competing with the rest of Western Europe to beat and torture the maximum profit out of Black bodies on plantations. Trying to understand the racial hierarchy of today without studying these origins is like trying to perform surgery without any medical knowledge.

Power Dynamics

The cannibal spirit unleashed by Europe on Africa went on to haunt relations between the two continents for the rest of history. Today, because racism is understood to be a blight on humanity, most Westerners don't openly brag about how much wealthier and more stable their societies are than many places in Africa. Instead, Western media and corporate culture like to celebrate international exchange of all kinds (usually in the context of selling things). But they can't hide the power dynamics between the West and the rest. The world's best Black and Brown athletes play for White countries – not the other way around. All images of Black people, positive or negative, are shared around the world using Western technology made from expropriated African materials. I used to have my head in the clouds, thinking that this interconnectedness could be used to make Africa as rich as the West. This was before I studied the situation, back when (like a lot of us do) I would reach shallow conclusions about Black issues just by looking around and taking the world at face value. Loads of us in Black communities joke about African dictators being greedy, and African parents being tough, and Black people not trusting each other and this and that. But when I finally got tired of guessing what our problem was, focused study revealed to me that, despite our flaws, Black people are all living in conditions dictated by White power. It makes me sick to think of all those who will never get the chance to look any further into history, due to a lack of time, money or opportunity.

If you open up a book halfway and start reading, you'll never fully grasp the story, no matter how many pages you get through. The story of Africa and Europe is, sadly, a story of one-way violence that plays out in our lives today. The point of this violence was first to extract African labour, then to control African land. Since this has gone so well for Europeans, the mission is now to keep Africans in positions that don't threaten the status quo. This oppression has been the norm for so long that many White leaders who really give it thought are quietly terrified that one day the tables will turn.

Human Sacrifice

Today's world was built on a racist division of labour dictated by a minority ethnic group from the Northern Hemisphere collectively known as Western Europeans. Growing up, I didn't even know this group was so much smaller in numbers than Africans or Asians, because their position in the world was never discussed, and their dominance was never questioned. Not in the mainstream anyway. Through slavery, European states made more money than they ever did from gold or silver. They weren't just violent to Africans either; in pursuit of land, Europeans killed 99 per cent of indigenous peoples in the Americas – directly, through murder, or indirectly, through disease – and ripped each other to shreds for control of slave colonies. This wasn't a blip; it was standard Western European practice for hundreds of years. Portugal controlled the sugar trade through the super-colony of Brazil, in which the racist division of labour had imported African slaves working day and night in factory-like concentration camps. This was the real foundation of Europe's Industrial Revolution, which was still a few centuries away at the time; huge numbers of workers funnelled into mechanised mass-production schemes, which were owned by a handful of people who controlled the capital that organised everyone else. Yet somehow, even at the highest stage of my education, this link between slavery and Western wealth was never discussed.

Erasure

European silence about slavery almost blinded me to the leading role Britain played. In 1625, while Portugal and Holland were fighting for control of the South Atlantic, England quietly set up shop in Barbados, soon becoming super-rich, surpassing Portugal as leader of the sugar trade and, eventually, global leader of the slave trade. The secret to Britain's success was African flesh. It blows my mind how Western Europeans focus so much on their cultural differences without ever seeing their similarities in the identical horrors they have inflicted on non-Europeans. Holland, for example, bullied Portugal out of Brazil in the early 1600s, while also grabbing hold of the Portuguese slave trade in Africa. This allowed them to ship over 30,000 Africans to the Americas in twenty years – literally copying Portugal's pattern. England later snatched Jamaica off Spain in 1655 and continued to sacrifice Africans for profit, in the exact same way as the Portuguese. When the enslaved Africans of Saint-Domingue, the 'greatest colony in the world' (as C. L. R. James framed it in *The Black Jacobins*[21]), fought off France for the twelve years from 1791 to 1803 to win their independence, the Spanish then invaded them and got beaten back. After that, 60,000 British soldiers tried invading again over five years and got the same result, before one more French attempt, which was also slapped down by the Africans. In the 1820s, the French got revenge for this humiliation through what Marlene Daut calls the 'greatest heist in history',[22] when France blackmailed Haiti (as it was by then known) with a debt of just under $30 billion in today's money – the price of diplomatic recognition by the country's former slaver. They claimed this penalty was for loss of earnings and property (i.e. slaves), but it also ensured Haiti's economy would never take off. If Haiti rejected the debt, it would be war – for ever – so the young nation accepted and spent the first 120 years of its life paying off the bill. As recently as 2015, France stated – for the millionth time – that it will not be repaying this criminal debt. And as recently as mid-2023, Haiti was in the news for an 'outbreak' of violence, lawlessness and disease. Not once in this news coverage have I heard any mention of France.

White Denial

It takes a particular kind of denial to erase the link between all that imperial domination and the current distribution of power and wealth across the world. White denial is the impulse to discredit Afrocentric explanations of history, and Britain is like the global centre of this tradition. This denial doesn't come from an innocent misunderstanding: it's from an irrational, egotistical insistence that Whiteness is just better than Blackness. Black Studies pioneer Kehinde Andrews describes it as the 'psychosis' of Whiteness – psychosis being a mental state of disconnection from reality. You can only read White denial in this way because of the trail of evidence that White supremacy has left behind. In *Born in Blackness,* Howard French highlights that up until 1820, the number of Africans that were transported across the Atlantic was four times bigger than the number of Europeans.[23] Why? Because African flesh was the key ingredient to Western development. The British Empire rose to power off the back of the wealth that those Africans provided. But all these centuries later, Britain still can't bring itself to say, 'Fair enough. We did that. We owe you.' White denial is not exclusive to White people, though. As recently as 2023, when asked by Labour MP Bell Ribeiro-Addy if his government would apologise for slavery and colonialism, Rishi Sunak, Britain's first non-White Prime Minister, gave the same response as Prime Ministers before him: no. Clearly, Britain has nothing to apologise for. In early 2022, speaking to the Carleton School of Journalism and Communication, Howard French used the following framing to explain the West's policy of distancing itself from the crimes it committed:

> The horror is so enormous . . . that it required of the peoples who founded these myths and who have made long careers across decades and centuries weaving fantasies . . . building literature . . . making Hollywood on the basis of these myths – it requires the erasure [of Africans' contribution] . . . the bad side of the story is so immense that it takes active suppression.[24]

The implications of such denial are far reaching. This is deeper than the inferiority complex that it breeds in the minds of Africans, who were shamelessly described by ex-French president Nicolas Sarkozy as never having 'fully entered into history'. The denial is tied to the platforming of Western culture as the pinnacle of humanity. It's a sick lie that is proving harder to hold onto as history unfolds.

Studying the Racial Hierarchy

It wasn't until my late twenties that I finally created my own reading plan, and confirmed what most of my Jamaican elders had been saying my whole life: today's racial hierarchy isn't the product of historical mistakes or unconscious bias – it's just pure evil. This period of reflection opened my eyes to how much time we, Black and Brown people, waste in Western education systems being drip-fed just enough information to participate in the Western workforce, while the Western forces working to keep our countries poor carry on unchallenged by the majority of us. As immigrants we're the tip of the iceberg – the few who made it to the rich part of the world, where we stay preoccupied with the challenge of survival. But the majority of any iceberg is under water and, in my case, that means hundreds of millions of Africans whose efforts, skills and sacrifices have little to no impact on their life chances. I slowly realised that growing up in the West, where Africa was rarely discussed or represented in any serious way, caused me to lose contact with the broader struggle. Flying back to Uganda every holiday season wasn't enough; I had no concept of African progress generally. I think most Black people over here see the big challenge of their lives as the journey to wealth, or family security. We have no mainstream spaces that encourage an international view of Black progress, and this mental, social and political detachment is ensured by our Western education.

13

White Supremacy

Recognition of African contributions to world history is crucial but, more than recognition, what's missing is the money. Africans were not sacrificed for nothing; European powers worked out that they could sidestep the normal rules of human conduct and grow money trees in stolen land by creating a new subhuman category for Africans, which would allow them to be worked like animals. They did this while fighting among themselves for freedom and human rights of their own. This process evolved into a system of world governance called imperialism.

Imperialism

One of the most frustrating things about discussing Black issues in a White country is the lack of awareness that this system is unnatural. In Britain, our curriculum is designed to present Western world domination as the result of hard work, unique cleverness and democracy, as if all those Black and Brown countries represented as poor in Western media are suffering from their own laziness, stupidity and selfishness. The crazy thing is, my time in Uganda has shown me that Africans often harbour these perceptions about each other too, with many unwilling to 'excuse' the blatant incompetence and short-sightedness of other Africans by 'blaming the White man'.

Under Eurocentric education and economic systems, it's almost impossible to convince some people that these behaviours can be programmed into a society through repeated sabotage, even through the country's basic design, which, in the case of Uganda, came from that apparently blameless White man. Unfortunately, the result of this teaching is pure arrogance. The kind of arrogance that convinced millions of voters that Britain would thrive without EU membership. The kind of arrogance that would deport Black Britons on the basis that they can't prove their Britishness. The kind of arrogance that caused the country to chase away the only popular member of their dying monarchy.

As far as I can see, it all comes down to money. Since the 1400s, European elites have invented new ways of extending the inequalities of their own regions to the world stage. By doing this, they invented a new *rock bottom* for even the poorest members of their societies to look down on. Slavery created a working class that these elites wouldn't have to pay for centuries. Then colonisation allowed the same elites to continue this injustice away from their home populations, which they framed as 'civilising' missions. This wasn't that long ago. More recently, over the past sixty years, neo-colonialism has enabled European elites to fund more comfortable lives for their own working classes by extracting labour and resources from former colonies under conditions of blackmail that would never be tolerated in their homelands. It's now reached the point where many White inheritors of this racist world order have lost track of the reason for all this: the money. With inequality in the West reaching levels that haven't been seen in over a hundred years, it can be easy for many in this hemisphere to forget that their world is so much richer than everywhere else. The logic that joins it all is imperialism.

And today, the most powerful institution upholding imperial logic is the nation state.

Settler Colonialism

Growing up, I was taught to think of myself as Ugandan, even though I lived in Britain. I didn't get the Western concept of nationality, so when I met Black people who saw themselves as English, I was baffled. Eventually it dawned on me that, to a lot of people, nationality wasn't necessarily an ancestral connection to a certain place; it was more a story about how you see yourself. For example, as a migrant who has moved from country to country, you might not identify with anywhere more than the country you grew up in, causing you to claim that nationality for the rest of your life, no matter where you end up. Alternatively, your travels might bring you to a place you connect with so strongly that you adopt a whole new nationality. For hundreds of millions of Black people, this question is more complicated than I could ever imagine. As a descendant of enslaved people, you might not identify with the nationality of your parents, grandparents or great-grandparents because, despite the real histories and traditions they co-developed, their situation was forced on them. So, what difference does it make if the world sees you as Caribbean? Or Latinx? Or American? Blood is thicker than borders.

On my journey through reimagining nationality, I noticed another group who should also find these issues complicated, but for some reason I had never heard them express any confusion about where they came from. I've talked a lot about Western Europeans and their global influence, but I haven't said much about their most divisive subcategory: settler colonisers. These are people who made new societies for themselves in other people's lands. Usually they didn't do this by asking permission. As I've already outlined, the desire to get rich without having natural wealth, big populations or the appetite for back-breaking labour led Europeans to transport Africans across the world and torture them for profit. I say 'Europeans' because it was literally Portugal, Spain, Holland, Britain and France who did it first. But a new subcategory arose out of these nations.

Settler colonialism led to Europeans forming nationalities on the basis of their overseas projects. In the case of North America, colonisation spun out of control. Collectively, Europeans killed off the indigenous owners of the land, then they fought among each other for ages. Britain beat up Holland on the East Coast (New York used to be New Amsterdam) and then confiscated parts of the Midwest, the South and Canada from France. During the seventeenth and eighteenth centuries, these growing states survived mainly by supplying the Caribbean colonies, which were booming from sugar and later cotton production (courtesy of enslaved Africans). This is how US nationality took shape – in the society that settlers formed, separate from Britain. They drew together in their frustration at being, as they saw it, *slaves* of the British monarchy. Seriously. These settlers were tired of being told how to trade and forced to pay taxes to an authority that wasn't even present, while they were the ones doing the hard work of murdering natives and driving slave labour. Kehinde Andrews's theory of Whiteness being a psychosis is the only way to explain why American settlers didn't see any contradiction in feeling enslaved by Britain, while enslaving Africans. What makes Andrews's theory so compelling is the fact that to this day, in spite of everything that is widely known about the violence of America's origins, the country still celebrates its 'Independence' Day as an anniversary of freedom from oppression, apparently oblivious to the colonising mission at its core.

White Nation-Building vs Black Nation-Building

The whitewashing of American history is so powerful that pioneers of African and Caribbean independence in the 1960s even likened their struggle to that of the early US. In her book *Worldmaking After Empire*, Professor Adom Getachew from the University of Chicago revisits efforts by Ghana's Kwame Nkrumah and Trinidad's Eric Williams to establish federations for their new states, like the US did in the late 1700s. The idea was that these young nations would be better off linking up with their neighbours, which both leaders calculated early on:

> At his speech during the Organization of African Unity Summit Conference in 1963 [Ghana's first president], Nkrumah likened the meeting of independent African states to the Philadelphia Congress. The delegates in 1787, he argued, did not yet see themselves as Americans. This identity 'was a new and strange experience,' but they still managed to act collectively.[25]

This chapter of Getachew's book helped me see identity as something that people sometimes build on purpose, out of common interests. She elaborates:

> Just as Americans had understood themselves as Pennsylvanians and Virginians, in 1963 delegates represented sovereign African states. Through union, African states

> could act collectively to secure their independence without the prerequisite that they understand themselves as a nation.

So, European colonisers in America had to come up with ways of pulling together against the threat of domination from outside, despite their differences – a challenge that Africans and Caribbeans were eventually faced with in the 1960s. Getachew provides more evidence of this thought process from Trinidad and Tobago's first Prime Minister, Eric Williams, to show how economic interests forced former colonies to think outside the box. She pulls up an unpublished 1963 essay in which Williams highlights the vulnerable position that forced America's European colonisers to create a new national identity: 'The colonies were condemned to an agricultural specialization, as they still are today in so many parts of the world . . .' i.e. early America was told what to trade and, effectively, how to live, just like poor countries of the 1960s (and today). In this essay, Williams insisted that economic ties would bring newly independent Caribbean nations together: 'Like the United States, the West Indies were composed of many peoples . . . their hope lay in securing their independence through union in a federation.'

To be fair, Nkrumah and Williams often referenced the US example with a little irony, using it to subtly pressure Europeans into accepting Third World self-determination. Getachew points out that America's situation only worked because it was a White supremacist power-grabbing project. She reminds us that '. . . neither Nkrumah nor Williams was naive about America's aspirations to global dominance.' Instead, 'by invoking a history of American anti-imperialism, both Williams and Nkrumah highlighted American hypocrisy in order to win the superpower to their cause.'

It didn't work. As Nkrumah suspected, America had already been instrumental in destabilising the newly independent Congo in 1960. This led to the murder of Patrice Lumumba, Congo's first democratically elected leader. Patrice was not that much older than I am now, bright-eyed and famously over-trusting of Americans. Apparently, he once shouted at a White diplomat over a misunderstanding and later apologised when he learned the guy was American, not Belgian. He explained that bad experiences with Belgian colonists made him wary of Europeans, but in Americans he saw fellow freedom fighters. At this time, the CIA was working on having him killed.

Meanwhile, back in Trinidad, Eric Williams found himself surrounded by countries living in fear of America's violent intolerance towards anything they didn't like. In March 1961, when announcing his multibillion-dollar ten-year aid programme, the *Alliance for Progress*, US president John F. Kennedy said, 'Let us once again awaken our American revolution until it guides the struggles of people everywhere – not with an imperialism of force or fear but the rule of courage and freedom and hope for the future of man.' But Malcolm X called him a trickster for a reason. Kennedy's interventions in Brazil, British Guyana, Colombia, Cuba, the Dominican Republic, Ecuador, Guatemala, Haiti, Peru and Venezuela directly contradicted all that freedom talk.

My point is that nation states as we know them came out of the European imagination. When Black people fought to build their own set-ups, White power said no. Nkrumah and Williams's failed federalist projects are just two examples. After mutilating Haiti in the nineteenth century, France spent the twentieth century trapping over 100 million Africans in a 'Union' that gave it control over African resources, militaries and economies . . . *after* these Africans gained independence from the

French empire. Since they were all neighbours, France was able to play the new nations against each other by rewarding or violating each according to their obedience. And thanks to Black History Month, we've all heard many times how hard the US fought to block African American freedom. After the end of legal slavery in the mid-1800s, millions of formerly enslaved Black people were forced to return to their oppressors for jobs. This obviously kept them poor and in constant danger of violence for another few generations. A hundred years later, the Jim Crow laws of the South became the focus of the new Civil Rights Movement, which imagined that racism could be overcome with new legislation. The clear limits of this concept pushed many African Americans to take seriously the earlier ideas of Jamaican activist Marcus Garvey, whose insistence on building Black-only enterprises and voluntarily moving back to Africa became the foundation of Black nationalism. In the Civil Rights era, Black nationalists such as Malcolm X and the Nation of Islam argued that it would be best for African Americans to form their own self-governed states, either on American land or (with the money owed to them by America for centuries of unpaid work) back in Africa. As I'm sure you're aware, none of these ideas were ever entertained by the White power structure.

The Threat of Non-White Self-Determination

The efforts of Kwame Nkrumah and Eric Williams in unifying African and Caribbean nations against colonialism were doomed by Western imperialism. It's not that either project would have been a guaranteed success; it's that they were never allowed to take off in the first place. The subtitle of Adom Getachew's *Worldmaking After Empire* is *The Rise and Fall of*

Self-Determination. The 'rise' was the wave of independence that climbed up from the end of World War One and reached its peak at decolonisation in the 1960s. The 'fall' was America stepping up as the new champion of White supremacy, taking over from a badly injured Europe, which it propped up with post-war recovery money, while unleashing hell on Black and Brown people at home and abroad. Although this rise happened over the course of the World Wars, and the fall unfolded during the Cold War, the West never needed a specific reason to dominate the global majority. Because of the racist division of labour that made Europeans so rich, it was easier for them to respect each other's rights than those of darker nations, even after cutting each other open, trying to exterminate other White people, and dragging those they oppressed into battle with them. It's not that Black and Brown people didn't have the willpower or the skills to organise themselves outside of Western control; it's that the West saw non-White self-determination as a threat.

If you still don't believe me, I understand. Through its dominant position across the media, Western culture promotes the same old-school idea of development that colonial conquest was built on: civilisation = shiny things. The West has a lot of shiny things that support its self-image as the winner of the world. All this wealth, technology and architecture must surely mean that, despite its mistakes, Western culture is ultimately the best, right? But there's another view of civilisation. Some people think that what matters most is how we treat each other. To many of us, a society that sacrifices human beings in the pursuit of shiny things can't claim to be superior to a less materialistic one in which every single life is valued.

When Black and Brown nations have attempted to build themselves up by investing in their own people, Western powers have repeatedly bombed, shot, poisoned and bribed the progressive spirit out of them. Throughout the twentieth century, capitalism was force-fed to underdeveloped nations through Western brutality and corruption. There were two levels of hypocrisy in this: firstly, imposing economic policies on these countries was the opposite of democracy – i.e. capitalism didn't 'win' by popularity, only through violence; secondly, the policies imposed were far more extreme than those practised by Western powers in their own countries, often contradicting them completely.

14

George the Worker

Earlier, we looked at two different ways of dealing with racism: Black liberalism and Black radicalism. A Black liberal believes racism will recede as Black people get more access to liberal society, while a Black radical believes that racism won't go away until society completely changes course. As you can probably gather from my life story up to university, I was a liberal. By the time I reached my early twenties, my head was full of education programmes I wanted to implement in my community. But although my heart was in the right place, I didn't understand how misguided my outlook was.

Rap and School

As an optimistic Cambridge graduate, my dream was to coach young Black people to do better in school, so that they could get well-paying jobs, return to their neighbourhoods and do the same. It was OK in theory, but we don't live in a theoretical world. Over the years I was forced to accept that the school-to-prison pipeline was often more powerful than any individual teacher. I came to understand the compromise that many teachers had already made; they knew they couldn't save everyone, so they focused on the children they *could* help. Even as I write this, the thought of good people being pressured by a bad system into making such compromises makes me sick. In theory, yes, the community and the education system (and everything else) would be much better if we as individuals all worked really hard to fix what was broken. But in reality, most of us are governed by a few, who have a vested interest in keeping things the way they are.

The more I started thinking in terms of *most* of us, instead of the few who might do well in school, the more my mind opened to new strategies for change. Some of these strategies were already in place and had been staring me in the face for years, waiting for me to see them for what they were. For example, my time in the UK Rap scene exposed me to the different ways in which people learn and discover their strengths. I watched my friends slowly master rhyming, complex storytelling, production technology, crowd control, information dissemination and more. On top of that, it was almost a rule that the most advanced rappers were kids who got kicked out of school, and to me, this was a clue. If the baddest kids were able to focus on Rap in a way that they couldn't in school, did Rap have an educational edge that school lacked? I believed it did, and the most important factor to me was language.

Rap is based on our own dialect, which carries its own authority. When we talk naturally, we are more confident, and that confidence allows us to commit. The reverse of this is an education system where the teachers, the textbooks and the exams use language that is imposed on us by a dominant class, discussing things that don't feel real to us. Even the literature this system wanted us to enjoy was handed down from previous generations of White men describing what they were going through, which we were expected to understand and write about enthusiastically. Most of us were able to force ourselves to do what was necessary for the grades, but we still felt constantly tricked by the complex rules and hidden traps of 'proper' English. Rap didn't do that. It accepted us as we were, allowing us to take in and share perspectives that we valued without being punished for having a good time. Rap provided an alternative space for us to grow in ways that were not possible in school. In the Rap scene, all those kids who got excluded felt confident that they belonged. They didn't mind not being the best or having to work hard and make sacrifices and continuously show up without any immediate rewards. By contrast, a classist education system produces diminishing returns for a young person who isn't sure they'll ever get anything out of school. As they grow older, the gap between what school expects of them and what they believe they can do seems to get wider and wider. Eventually, feelings of alienation harden into resentment and contempt. By the time we were sixteen, many of my peers sneered at the idea of showing up to their exams but, funnily enough, they always respected me for doing so.

So, in my early twenties, I had a head full of schemes about using Rap to educate. All I knew was that the generation after me had no mentors who took both Rap and school to their furthest extent, so we had no idea what they might achieve with this kind of mentorship. I believed (and still believe) that we could use everything Rap taught us about interpreting the world in our own language, and apply it to interpreting any course material. How did I hope to prove this? I planned to rhyme whole modules, collaborate with artists from different fields, create new literature about our history – anything to spark young imaginations. But nothing could happen without money and, for me, that's where the real education started.

The 'Business' Part of the Music Business

In the years after graduation, I learned things about money that forced me to put my Rap plan on the back burner. One day, towards the end of my time with Island Records in 2015, I asked the label to show me how much they had spent on me so far. I was shocked. For that amount we could have funded a number of music-based educational programmes for a decade. What made it worse, in my opinion, was that this money had been poured into things that didn't make me stand out – things that downplayed the fact I was the only musical poet of my kind in the whole country, and pushed me to compete along the same lines as everyone else. All these years later, I have to credit Island for giving me first-hand insight into corporate logic. They would rather spend all that money on a familiar formula, which might provide one commercial success out of a thousand failures, than take on a truly entrepreneurial challenge to improve society. But why was I surprised? Capitalism has always been like this.

The 'capital' in capitalism refers to anything that is used to produce wealth – like machines in factories or, back in the day, enslaved Africans on plantations. In my case, the record label provided capital in the form of money to cover my recording process and living costs (in theory). The capital I provided was my own work ethic, which would turn my thoughts into poetry. Even though the label's money and my efforts were both needed to create the final product, I soon learned that not all assets are created equal.

Technically, my work ethic was as important to this record deal as the finance from the record company, if not more. Without the label, I had poems and an audience, but no upfront investment. Without me, the label had its existing business and no foothold in the new genre I represented. But in reality, Island Records was bigger and more powerful than me, and was therefore able to dominate our relationship. I still remember the day I signed. My lawyer, a kind-hearted music lover called Zubin, wasn't happy because he and the lawyer from Island still hadn't clarified the difference between the musical work I would deliver under contract and my original spoken word poetry, which would be left out of the deal. We all agreed there would be a difference, but it was hard to say exactly what that difference was. Zubin's concern was that the label would completely control my brand, which they didn't yet understand. This would be risky because, by that point, I had gained a national following for doing something completely new. From Zubin's time in the music industry, he knew there was a high chance a major record label would undervalue my creativity and kill my momentum. But, since the deal was what I wanted, the most he could do was carve out parts of my career that Island Records couldn't touch. So, when Darcus, the label's president, set a date for the signing while these questions remained unresolved, Zubin wisely advised me to go slow. But being young and naive, I didn't get it. I got swept up in the champagne and celebrations and just signed the contract, not fully appreciating what I'd just done.

Before long I would return to that document, this time slowly taking in every word, trying to understand what went wrong. The first red flag came when, out of frustration with the label's half-stepping, I uploaded my own song, 'If the Shoe Fits', to my own YouTube channel. We'd had lots of meetings about this song and everyone at Island gave it the green light, yet every time we agreed to get the ball rolling, nothing happened. So, imagine my surprise when I uploaded the track, only to have it removed within hours on the grounds of a copyright breach.

Apparently, this recording belonged to Universal Music Group, the parent company of Island Records, and I wasn't authorised to share 'their' intellectual property. I was fuming. I pulled up the contract and there it was, in one stupidly long sentence full of bad grammar:

> . . . the Artist [me] assigns to the Company [Island Records] with full title guarantee and **the Company is the sole and exclusive owner of the entire copyright and all rights of action and all other rights of every kind** (including all performers' property rights) in and to the Recordings, Films, Artwork and Artist Website Materials (whether those rights are now known or in the future created) to which the Artist is now or at any time after the date of this agreement becomes entitled by virtue of or under any of the laws in force in any part of the Territory to hold to the Company, its successors and assigns absolutely for the Territory and for the whole period of those rights for the time being capable of being assigned by the Artist together with any and all renewals and extensions and thereafter (insofar as possible) in perpetuity.

So, in English: from the date of my signing, Island owned anything and everything I recorded, up until I had fulfilled my end of the deal. On top of that, they owned my image. The funny thing is, I knew this already because Zubin had carefully explained it all to me, but it took this situation to make the cold, complicated words of the contract become real in my mind. I kicked up a fuss at the label over my song being removed, and they reversed the decision. But the song never did get a proper release, and I continued to be ignored for a while after that.

Another red flag came when I presented a different song to the label. Out of respect for my collaborators and fans who really cherished it, I won't mention the song's name, but in honesty this one was inferior to 'If the Shoe Fits' in every way. To be fair, it was meant to be a simpler offering, since I wanted to test my audience's reaction to completely different styles. 'If the Shoe Fits' was an experimental piece of musical storytelling; its whole purpose was to introduce the listener to a new version of my poetry. Along with two of my favourite producers, Miles and Jojo (then known as The Confectionery), I went on a year-long journey to figure out each layer of the record, which didn't have any conventional song structure to guide us. At times, we got lost and scrapped the whole thing, returning to a blank page after months of work. But eventually we created an undisputed masterpiece and established a unique style that fans are *still* pressing me to return to.

By contrast, this new song took a matter of minutes. The music was unimaginative, and I didn't think too much about the lyrics – specifically because I had already taken the over-thinking approach with my other songs. I challenged myself to write something relaxed, and imagined I would release it later down the line, once people had taken in my more intense work. Nowadays, it makes me laugh when I recollect the label's reaction to this song, but at the time I didn't find it funny. They acted like I'd struck gold. One person in particular kept congratulating me on 'finally figuring it out', dancing around the room like money was falling from the sky. I remember thinking one of us is crazy, because this song is undeniably basic. Still, I had no choice but to play along. At this point, Island had dragged their feet so much that I was desperate to use any record to negotiate the release of ones I really loved. And it worked. The label agreed to release this one as well as the seven other tracks that continued the story I'd started on 'If the Shoe Fits'. Truthfully, I believed these songs were good enough to be presented as my official album, but Island wouldn't go for that, so I downgraded them to an extended play record, or an 'EP', which is like a junior version of an album. I called it *The Chicken and the Egg* EP, referring to the cycle of premature parenthood that the songs explored. Island ended up throwing its weight behind the basic song, and doing nothing to support *The Chicken and the Egg*, which I was forced to release for free online, with no marketing. This was by far the lowest point of my career.

What did I learn? Not all assets are created equal. Island Records brought the finance, and I brought the work, but one overpowered the other. My record deal gave me 'creative control', an empty term used to reassure me that I was in the driver's seat, but when decisions had to be made, Island's money got the final say. All my hard work and commitment couldn't match up to the record company's ability to turn the volume up or down using their control of the budget. Not to mention the fact I had handed over all my rights to them, which has always been a non-negotiable part of most record deals. But as much as I grew to resent Island, I was more angry at myself. I'd spent the last year of university studying both capitalism in general and the creative industries in particular. Island did everything my studies told me they would do, but despite calculating the risk I was taking on prior to signing, I hadn't factored in one crucial aspect of human behaviour: manipulation.

The only reason I signed with Island was because the label's Black leaders convinced me we were committed to the same cause. But in the end, they were committed to profit, which explains how they got to the top of the music industry in the first place. It's not that I assumed the colour of their skin made them trustworthy; it's that they worked on me for months, talking history and heritage. They knew exactly who I was, and what I needed to hear at twenty-two years old, so they never talked about fame or money – only about the impact I could have in the lives of oppressed people, given the right platform. Yet when I produced innovative material designed to make that impact, they themselves shut it down – not necessarily because they were bad people, just because they didn't know how to sell it. This was what I'd read about in Cambridge: the influence of the profit motive in the creative industries. Owners of capital wanted to maximise profits, so they preferred products that were easy to sell and mass-produce. This whole industry relied on a few players having enough money to take on the financial risk of supporting new, unproven artists. But those players preferred non-disruptive, unchallenging music over anything that was hard to define, like my new hybrid genre. The Island Records team couldn't just say that, though; they had to promise the opposite in hopes of capturing my buzz, converting me into a popstar and buying me off with fame. If their strategy had worked, it would have crushed my chances of changing anything, because my success would have been based on fitting in.

My short time in the music business was a painful but necessary learning experience; I had so much theory in my head, all that was missing was some real-world practice. Despite the critical acclaim that *The Chicken and the Egg* went on to enjoy, despite the BRIT Award and BET Award nominations it earned me, despite the sold-out tour and countless festival appearances that followed, it had been made clear to me that I was an insignificant worker in a big corporation. Record deals are funny because they pretend to treat artists like business partners, when really, they're workers without security. These deals say, 'Take this money', which is supposed to last over an unconfirmed period of time, 'and come back with music that sounds like what our competition is doing, but better. And don't do anything else with your life.' They offer short-term funding in exchange for all your long-term potential, which the label shapes according to its narrow aims. If you don't play along, they withhold the money, or worse. I saw top-selling artists with vicious drug habits funded by the industry. Some of the most talented people I've ever met had mental breakdowns because of what the industry put them through. They lost confidence and, in some of the saddest cases, lost their love of music. I got off lightly; eventually I just asked to leave and to Darcus's credit, he let me. Still, to this day, I don't believe any other industry could have given me a clearer picture of how the world really works.

15

Member of the British *What*?

The racial abuse I get following appearances on the politics talk show *Question Time* is nothing compared to what I received when I publicly turned down an honour from the Queen. Let's skip ahead in my story to December 2019 (we'll come back to the original timeline later). After having independently released the first chapter of my audio-series *Have You Heard George's Podcast? (HYHGP)* the previous year with my friend and producer, Benbrick, I was now releasing Chapter Two – this time with the BBC – and it ended with a shock revelation. Months earlier, in May of 2019, I got a call from someone telling me I'd been nominated for the 'Queen's Honours'. I didn't know what this meant, so I googled it. Here's what the official website said:

> As 'fountain of honour' in the UK, The Queen has the sole right of conferring titles of honour on deserving people from all walks of life, in public recognition of their merit, service or bravery.

I was being recognised by the monarchy for my work and would receive a letter containing the details shortly, according to the voice on the phone. Sure enough, the letter came and there it was – my name next to the title 'MBE': Member of the Order of the British Empire. Honestly, I felt a rush. My ego swelled up as I thought, *I'm only twenty-eight*. Wiley, the man who invented Grime, had only been awarded an MBE the year before, in 2018. I gave myself permission to feel proud, as I usually have such a stoic approach to work that it catches me off guard when I'm being celebrated. Just weeks prior, it was announced that *Have You Heard George's Podcast?* was nominated for seven British Podcast Awards – a record that will probably stand for ever since they created a rule to stop it happening again lol. And despite a nasty run-in with police the previous year, I was deeper in my Black liberal celebrity mindset than I realised. I felt confident about my place in Britain. You can hear this confidence on Episode 12 of *HYHGP* 'A Night to REMember'. This was the first thing I wrote for the second chapter of the series, and it reflects my headspace at the time. I characterised Britain as a woman I call 'Brit':

> Brit, honestly . . . I owe you an apology.
> You've done a lot for me, and I don't think I've thanked you properly.

I did feel thankful towards Britain, and I still do. But I also feel other things. Those things started flooding my mind over the twenty-four hours following the MBE call. I remember going over the words '*member* . . . of the *British Empire*'. It was the first time I really thought about it. To commend me for my work, and thank me for making the country look good, the empire was 'honouring' me by recognising my 'membership'. I had no problem with the British Podcast Awards honouring me because they didn't make it weird. This empire thing was making it weird. Why the title? I went back over the letter, and this time I noticed something. The 'honour' came with a condition: it could be taken away if I got into trouble – which I read as 'if we change our mind'. That line helped me sober up quick; this was a contract. For the privilege of letting this empire claim me, I got to wear its logo like a badge of honour next to my name. And as a subtle way of keeping me in my place, the empire gave me this honour on the condition that it could be withdrawn. But what was honourable about that? If you honour me by buying this book, does that make me a member of whatever you've got going on? If I honour you for taking the time to read this book, should I stamp my initials on you to make it real? To be appreciated is an honour, but branding is just branding.

I'll admit, my knowledge on the British Empire wasn't up to scratch at this time. I knew it was exploitative, but I'd also heard a lot of Ugandans talking about how much better things were in the colonial era. On top of that, Western media peddles imperialist propaganda religiously, so, without even paying attention, I've probably taken in pro-empire messages my whole life. *The Crown* is still a popular TV show, recruiting fans for the monarchy every season. *The Jungle Book* is still an undeniable classic, keeping alive the name of its arch-racist author, Rudyard Kipling, who also wrote *The White Man's Burden* and other tributes to empire. Anyway, isn't the empire the Commonwealth now? Didn't everyone get independence and move on? Although I recognised the need to brush up on my knowledge of the British Empire, I knew I couldn't accept the MBE. The choice was already made for me by the wording of this 'honour'. I wasn't necessarily anti-monarchy at this time, but I wasn't about to co-sign the whole idea of empire by attaching those words to my name.

What was the British Empire?

The British Empire started off as a global system of wealth-extraction for Britain's ruling class, and over the centuries this has taken different forms. The ruling class includes landowning families, influential merchants, powerful politicians and the monarchy. These were the original financers of overseas efforts to keep power and wealth flowing towards Britain. Those efforts sometimes started off as mutual trade relationships, but often descended into armed robbery. In the early 1600s, the English invaded Ireland, enslaved its people and forced them to work on plantations at the dawn of capitalist development. A couple of decades later, the country claimed Barbados for itself in the face of intense competition from the Netherlands, Portugal, Spain and France. This was in the 1620s, during the period known as the 'first' British Empire. A century and a half later, in the 1770s, the empire suffered a devastating loss; some of its oldest, most populous colonies on the American mainland broke away to form the United States, as settlers grew to hate the British government for controlling how they traded (and therefore, how they lived). However, decades before this split, Britain seized control of the Indian subcontinent through moves made by the privately owned East India Company. Dominating such a huge portion of Asia brought immense privilege to Britain, and the loss of America caused the superpower to lean into this privilege, hailing the dawn of the 'second' British Empire. Clashes with France in the early 1800s cemented Britain's place as the strongest imperial power in the world. The period after this, between 1815 and 1914, is sometimes referred to as 'Pax Britannica' (peace in Britain), because the country was relatively stable; but for the parts of the world that Britain was moving into, this era was far from peaceful.

Empire and Asia

As they colonised Asia throughout the nineteenth century, the British continued their old pattern of wealth creation: using corporations like the East India Company to extract capital from a separate race of workers, and using that capital to invest in their own development. At the heart of this Asian operation was British India, which originally included Pakistan, Bangladesh, Burma and more. India generated extreme wealth for the British under a violent regime of repression and impoverishment for the Indian people. In a conversation with Economics Professor Michael Hudson for her book *Geopolitical Economy*, political scientist Radhika Desai explains that Britain's colonial profits

> . . . came from taxing the empire, and . . . from the massive surpluses that the empire ran with the rest of the world, where these poor people . . . were working their guts out to produce the cotton, the tea, the coffee, the rice, the wheat . . . which was exported to the rest of the world, while often people starve . . . and it was . . . earning for Britain the surpluses which it exported . . . to North America, to South Africa . . . to the colonies, and to Europe.[26]

Empire and Slavery

This was an updated form of British slavery – the work-from-home version. Meanwhile, decades into the 1800s, Africans in Britain's West Indian colonies were still enslaved the old way, despite Britain having abolished the slave trade in 1807. Slavery was still legal, and it was still hell on Earth, so rebellions erupted repeatedly, such as the 1823 uprising in Demerara in British Guyana, in which the enslaved Africans were eventually overpowered, imprisoned and murdered by the British. Many uprisings saw similar outcomes, making it harder and harder for the ruling class to whitewash Britain's brutality with claims of moral superiority over those it ruled. This clash between Britain's self-image and its unmasked gangsterism created a real problem for Brits who didn't exclude Africans from their newly formed ideas of universal human rights. When 60,000 Africans in Jamaica rose up on the last days of 1831, led by the Black Baptist deacon Sam Sharpe, British authorities, again, responded violently. And although this uprising didn't directly free the enslaved, the subsequent trial paved the way to the official end of slavery.

It's important to understand that the moral character of Britain's ruling class was unchanged by these events. The British government actually took out a loan worth £20 billion in today's money in order to compensate slaveholders for their loss of earnings. Former British Prime Minister and current Foreign Secretary David Cameron and his wife, Samantha, are both related to recipients of this money. James Duff, son of one of David's ancestors, was an army officer and MP in the 1700s, and received today's equivalent of £3 million in compensation for the loss of over 200 slaves. According to the *Guardian*, a similar amount was paid to one of Samantha's ancestors for 164 slaves in St Lucia.[27] These links are not exclusive to the Camerons – they were normal among England's ruling class, because these people didn't see the enslavement of Africans as a moral issue, which explains the next phase of British-African contact. Still, this shameful reality didn't stop David Cameron from brushing off Jamaica's calls for reparations in September of 2015 by telling the Jamaican Parliament to get over it.

Empire and Africa

By the mid-1800s, Europeans had established a firm presence on the West African coast. This was done using the usual sequence of colonisation: trade, followed by armed robbery. Their presence was a disaster twice over; not only did the European addiction to African flesh drain the populations of African kingdoms, weakening their ability to develop, but Europeans also undermined African society in the long run by stoking regional conflicts for access to slave labour. Anyway, by the mid-1800s, they had only managed to go so far into the actual continent. Europeans' poor understanding of hygiene in the tropical terrains of Africa led to high mortality rates among the first colonisers who tried to move deeper inland. In 1847, when the Hungarian scientist Ignaz Semmelweis proved that doctors could save lives by washing their hands, the whole scientific community rejected him. They actually had him locked up in an asylum – that's how badly they didn't want to wash their hands. Nevertheless, as they progressed, Europeans found new routes along important waterways that sharpened their interest in the continent.

By the 1870s, explorers like John Speke, Henry Stanley and Pierre Savorgnan de Brazza had seriously improved Western access to Africa by mapping the Central African Great Lakes and rivers. At this point, capitalism in Britain was under pressure from its never-ending need to expand, causing a trade deficit that pushed the empire to find new markets. This issue was being felt across Europe in general, on top of the fact that industrial growth created high demand for raw materials like rubber, palm oil and diamonds. Africa provided the perfect solution to both problems. The 1880s kicked off with Western powers grabbing different parts of the continent, leading to the

Berlin Conference of 1884–5. At this conference, which was held in the German city of Berlin, Europeans drew up an agreement on the partitioning of Africa. Britain, along with Austria-Hungary, Denmark, France, Germany, Italy, Norway, the Ottoman Empire, Portugal, Russia, Spain, Sweden-Norway and the United States, sent diplomats to the conference and signed the legislation it produced: the Berlin Act. This was a defining moment in what became known as the 'scramble for Africa'.

And at this point, I'd like to pass on some advice that a thoughtful person once gave me: if you haven't already done so, make time in your life to read Walter Rodney's *How Europe Underdeveloped Africa*.[28] Rodney was a Black freedom fighter from British Guyana. He wasn't known for violence, yet his teachings on African history and class struggle were enough to get him banned from Jamaica, leading to riots that ended the lives of six people. Rodney was only twenty-six at the time. For his belief that Guyanese society should overcome ethnic divisions through class solidarity, he was harassed by authorities in his own country, and eventually blown to bits by a car bomb, widely believed to have been orchestrated by the government. For obvious reasons, *How Europe Underdeveloped Africa* is largely ignored in the West, but it will give you an understanding of the well-planned devastation this period brought to the continent, for the purpose of enriching the West. The book is phenomenal, not just for its analysis but for the fact that Rodney was just thirty years old when he released it. Like Eric Williams's *Capitalism and Slavery*, as well as C. L. R. James's *The Black Jacobins*,[29] this groundbreaking book stands as a reminder of how hard Black people have worked to set the record straight about Africa and her children. It contradicts the lie that young Black minds can't be motivated to study and organise; in fact, the resistance to these efforts actually highlights the White supremacist fear of Black radical potential. Whereas I believe everyone should read Rodney's work, this one is especially important for all my Black readers. I don't care how long it takes – make sure you do it. Without the insight provided by this book, it's very hard to discuss Africa's issues in a serious way.

16

Maybe They're All One

After leaving my record deal, I needed a change of direction. My time in the music industry helped me clarify the whole point of my career; I wanted a public platform to support oppressed people that wasn't controlled by anyone else. Some members of my family later admitted to me that they didn't have a clue what I was thinkng by walking away from the label. They thought I was too hot-headed (which I might have been) and worried that the pressure of delivering music was the true reason why I left. They weren't the only ones. I'm sure that, from the outside looking in, the industry seems all-powerful, efficient and professional, causing people to believe that any artist is better off with it than without, despite the endless horror stories of robbery and mental abuse that it produces. But by the time I left, that image meant nothing to me. I assured my family that, as long as I could write poems, I'd have a future somewhere in the media; the challenge was now figuring out where that would be.

After binge-watching *The Wire*, undeniably the greatest show I've ever seen, I felt a strong urge to try writing for TV. First, I wanted something like *Russell Howard's Good News*, a British show that broke down the news of the week in a stand-up set by comedian Russell Howard, with a few funny sketches and special guests. I liked that Russell used his comedy to talk about the world critically, because I had always wanted to do the same with my poetry. Over time, I started discussing ideas with an associate I'd met on a previous job. We'll call him Joe. Joe was one of those creatives who was organised, punctual and entrepreneurial. His mind overflowed with ideas, and he had an impressive record of executing them in ways that brought talented people together. We met before I signed to Island Records, collaborating on a documentary about young creatives. While I was signed to Island, Joe watched from afar, happy for my progress. After I left, we reconnected and I updated him on the creative struggles I had experienced, while he shared the impressive work he'd been doing in the theatre world. He also shared that he was a big fan of *The Chicken and the Egg* EP and appreciated the storytelling above all else.

Joe encouraged me to look into theatre, and eventually TV. He introduced me to his friend at a production company that made big shows for the BBC and ITV. We'll call her Meg. Although my original idea was this Russell Howard kind of factual show, Meg worked in the fiction department – the part where they make TV dramas. It would be wrong to say Joe and Meg influenced me to change my concept, since I was open to trying drama as well. This new concept would be to tell my story through a drama series that allowed me to analyse the world critically, like I do with this book. Why? For years, I had been avoiding placing my personal life at the centre of my work. I always thought that approach was a stumbling block for Black artists because we are often told the same old story, tricking ourselves into thinking we're changing the narrative because it's 'our turn'. Since we live in similar conditions, we end up painting similar pictures; but our job should be building a new world, not artistically reproducing the old one. I still struggle with this, but I've learned to compromise . . . I think.

Developing this new concept with Joe, Meg and her team was fun. They listened to my story and shaped it into the outline of a TV show. After this process, the plan was to try and sell that outline to a network. Thankfully, we received interest quite quickly, so the time soon came for us all to have the 'business' chat. This was backwards. We should have had that chat at the start, but I clearly hadn't learned my lessons from the music industry. Joe and Meg made a big deal about me being credited as *Creator*, *Writer* and 'star' of the show, but I wanted one more role: *Producer*. Or at least *Associate Producer*. Research told me this was my only way of guaranteeing control of the creative process, since producers were basically shot-callers. One thing I did learn from Island was the difference between 'talent' and 'executive'. What would be the point of giving these guys my life story if I had no say in how the casting, locations, wardrobe, the whole damn budget was handled? When I raised this, Meg and Joe reassured me that I *was* in control. 'George, you're the writer *and* star of your own show,' they would say. 'No network wants an unhappy star. We're all working to deliver your vision!' Unfortunately for them, I had music industry PTSD, and the familiar sound of empty corporate promises that directly contradicted their business methods sent me into a panic. I had been open with Meg about my trouble at the label, so when she told me it was 'impossible' for a similar situation to arise on our project, I sent her the recent example of 'Roll Safe'.

Roll Safe, or RS, was a character created by actor, comedian and writer Kayode Ewumi. I first noticed him on my social media feed in 2015, just after I had left the record deal. Kayode himself played this fake-it-'til-you-make it young Black man, roaming around his area trying to make something out of nothing. In the early social media days, Roll Safe appeared, like a lot of online comedians, in short, hilarious clips depicting awkward situations. The nuances of this character were so advanced, so specific to our generation (and our lives on council estates) that it would be easy for many to miss the humour but Roll Safe strongly reminded me of people from my childhood. Kids who constantly felt intimidated and inadequate in our volatile world, and coped by bluffing *hard*. These kids often said the wrong thing, embarrassed themselves and tried to play off their mistakes as intentional or insignificant. I'm sure every environment has people like this – in fact, I'm sure we've all been in situations where we've come across like this – but Kayode's acting made Roll Safe one hundred per cent believable. On 11 October 2015, he surprised us by releasing a twenty-two-minute YouTube video called *Hood Documentary*, directed by Tyrell Williams. It's not often that a social media act transitions so successfully into a longer-form scripted character. Kayode seemed to improvise his way through a number of scenes in which Roll Safe is followed around by a camera crew. I was crying with laughter from the first few lines, which reveal that RS has misunderstood the project he is being filmed for. With a proud smile, he states to the camera that he's 'being documented for Independent', and we assume he means the *Independent* newspaper. When the director corrects him, saying, 'No . . . I'm an independent film-maker,' he can't hide his disappointment, and it suddenly becomes clear to the viewer that the guy is clueless. For the next twenty minutes, Kayode expertly moves between different scenarios, all of which reveal more of RS's delusional but likeable persona. *Hood Documentary* was an overnight hit. Everyone was quoting their favourite lines and before long it reached 1 million views. A few weeks later, Kayode and Tyrell followed up with a second, equally funny episode, proving that this wasn't a fluke – they had something different. And then the BBC got involved.

I've had some great experiences with the BBC, and I have a lot of respect for Kayode, but I was disappointed with their collaboration. It's hard to tell who was responsible for what, since I don't have insight into their production process but, regardless, the sharpness of Kayode's initial creation in contrast to the dullness of this BBC version convinced me that Kayode wasn't the problem. When we, the original fans, found out that the BBC had commissioned six episodes of *Hood Documentary*, many of us were happy but nervous. Like I said, it was a nuanced thing, and it had subtle humour that we had never seen in our image on mainstream British TV before. As Black people, we often feel the need to adjust our language and jokes in the presence of White people, and there was a good chance this would happen to Roll Safe. In my opinion, our fears were confirmed when the new series launched. In an email to Meg about why I needed to be a producer on my own show, I explained that the new characters, less improvisational script, smoother camerawork and cultural inconsistencies made this version of *Hood Documentary* feel very 'BBC'. Basically, it felt like White people wrote it. Yet, as I acknowledged in the email, the comments on the BBC Three YouTube channel were mostly positive. In fact, after a few minutes of scrolling just now, I could only find two comments that mirrored my thoughts. Here's the first one, from a viewer named dyingllama1:

> The low budget documentary feel and semi believable plot of the original two episodes made them much more hilarious. BBC – I'm glad you're promoting RS but don't turn this into another one of your moist programs!

It's like they tapped into my internal monologue. RS, in my opinion, was funnier when he was less refined. Steadier shots, too many actors and a script that had clearly gone through the corporate machine all changed the pace, delivery and context of his jokes. Here's the second comment that spoke my mind, from a viewer called ShynAwkward:

> Corporations always seem to take the life & soul out of creative expression.
> Just like a girlfriend who tries to change everything about her boyfriend until the things that she initially liked about him are gone – then they break up!
> The humour was in the rawness, but when corporate folks are involved, they always polish/sanitize things until the edge is gone :-(

This one is my favourite because that girlfriend analogy is priceless. 'More' isn't always 'better', but although the BBC isn't a private business, it still can't escape the logic of capital – like most of us – and capital says 'more *is* better'. In my unqualified opinion, the BBC sold Kayode the idea that a higher production budget would elevate his material. Of course, it's possible that he feels this series was his best work, in which case we can agree to disagree. But back in 2016, all I knew was that no corporation would put me in that position again. The logic of capital – in this case, that *more* viewers on a culturally compromised product is a *better* result than a smaller (but growing) audience with an authentic product – is not my kind of logic. Neither is the idea that the people with the money always know what's best. As I explained above, Black cultural work is more important than we think. We can't let these things slide; there's too much at stake.

Sadly, Joe and Meg begged to differ. They insisted that no network would give me a *Producer* credit because I didn't have the experience. I pointed out that my experience was the TV show we were trying to sell. I felt they continued acting like this didn't count, like the rules of becoming a producer were holy laws that couldn't be broken and, after a heated conversation with Joe, I walked away from the project. It was a simple decision but not an easy one. We'd spent months working on this and I still don't know if Joe and Meg actually understood where I was coming from. But, so what? They weren't making sense. In the music industry, I learned that without control of the budget, your project can be delayed or cancelled before it even gets off the ground. I also learned that the whole business relies on naive young people accepting bad deals under the influence of smooth-talking older people. So, watching these seasoned professionals from another industry apparently trying to finesse me into the same position I ended up in at Island Records made me feel like it was time to get the hell out of there. Maybe the reasons behind this are not so random. Maybe holders of capital have a habit of trying to reproduce the world they want to see at the expense of others. Maybe they're all one.

PART IV

History Rhymes

17

A New Wave

'Uncle George . . . when you were born, why did they call you "Uncle"?'

I closed my eyes and smiled. These were the moments I hoped to be present for when I decided to spend more time with my family that year. I explained to my nephew, Nicholas, that 'Uncle' was a special name I took on when *he* was born. His face turned thoughtful as he went over my answer in his head, before smiling and digesting it. I was exiting my teens when my cousin gave birth to Nicholas, and not much older when his little brother Malachi arrived. It wasn't until I got to university that I found out White people don't refer to their cousins' children as nephews and nieces – apparently, they're classed as 'third' cousins or something. I never understood it. I joked with my White friends that my logic on this one probably sounded as strange to them as theirs did to me. With my nephews, I always had fun being old enough to take the parental initiative but young enough to act like a kid if I felt like it. Honestly, though, during the Island years I didn't see them enough, and by the time I left the industry I had a growing concern that I was missing those precious years when they would still ask questions like, 'Why did they call you "Uncle"?' This feeling gnawed away in the back of my mind as their speech got less and less childlike. *Peppa Pig* was replaced by the *Minions*. *Paw Patrol* was replaced by *Spider-Man*. Alarm bells went off in my head when Malachi finally started pronouncing 'Spider-Man' properly (he used to say 'Fider-Man'), so I decided to rearrange my priorities.

By the end of 2016 I was burned out. While TV ads and corporate commissions paid the bills, I used this post-record-deal-window to experiment extensively, leaving me with little time to myself. Over the year I had travelled to America for the first time with Sentebale, the charity that Prince Seeiso of Lesotho co-founded with Prince Harry, who asked me to become an ambassador; I had collaborated with Chase & Status on their single, 'Spoken Word', which – according to all the social media posts I'm still tagged in – went on to become a gym classic; I had released my own song, 'Wake Up', with the production duo Devolution, and had a great time shooting the video in Uganda (produced by Kemiyondo Coutinho, shot by Isaac Oboth and featuring Lamic Kirabo); somewhere between all of that, with the help of my then manager Chisara Agu-Franklynn, I toured the UK independently, supported by The Compozers – thanks to the guys and everyone who came out! Oh yeah – and I also co-developed a TV show about my life that I wasn't able to get a production credit on. But while my enthusiasm for TV had cooled off a bit, I clearly still had one foot in music, even though I wasn't sure it was what I wanted. I was sure, however, that I missed my family, and I missed Uganda. I had started the year with a long break in the country and was more in love with it than ever. UG had always been the place that refocused me, calmed my spirit and brought contentment. Some advised me not to get caught up, though. They told me to concentrate on my life in the UK because Uganda would always be here. To me, it wasn't that simple. Since I didn't grow up there, I felt a strong urge to establish a foundation in Africa before I was too tied down elsewhere. But at the same time, I took pride in the progress I'd made so far.

Seven years prior, I was completely new to the country. Now, due to the amount of time I'd invested since, the place wasn't so foreign to me. I had a feel for Kampala culture that would assist me in slowly developing material relevant to my counterparts out there. This was super important because it was the most likely way to ensure I had a foothold in the country. Still, I knew there was unfinished business waiting for me in Britain . . . I just didn't know what Britain and I could offer each other.

Now that I was mainly out of the music industry, my mind was free to think in broader terms about where I was heading. I had gradually started coming around to the possibility that no one knew what to do with me and, on one hand, this was kind of exciting but on the other, it was daunting; it meant I'd have to come up with a completely original plan. The key to unlocking this plan lay at the heart of one big question: *what was the point of my poetry?* Was it to entertain? To educate? To earn? I had a strong feeling the answer was somewhere in between these three poles but, without a blueprint, all I could do was invest in my own ideas until something clicked. By this point, I'd had enough corporate experience to understand that no one would pay me to figure out my purpose, so I decided to be my own backer. Any money I earned would go towards my research and development process, and any poems I released would feed into one bigger plan. This was different from my path as a recording artist. In that role, the aim was to release all sorts of songs until one connects with the masses. Once that happens, you lean into whatever the masses like, and repeat. It's not a bad plan. When it works, it can generate residual income, buying you more time to do other things in the long run. But for me it would involve too much trial and error with too little intellectual discipline. It's hard to write songs for the mainstream while your mind is on structural change. Bob Marley was able to do it, but he was supported by a religion that was all about structural change, in a country that was going through nothing but structural change.

So, I used 2017 to experiment at a calmer pace, prioritising family time, reading more, following the news and observing the culture – generally, becoming an *active listener*. Since I had identified the need to educate as part of my purpose, I felt a responsibility to expand my understanding of the world before releasing more poetry. If I didn't do this, I'd probably end up repeating myself or sticking to familiar concepts that wouldn't change anything. I mentioned earlier my frustration with the model of creativity many of us start off with – using your life experience as the only reference for your art. Some people are great at this, but without actively looking for new ideas you're likely to go around in circles, thematically. Relationships, money, vibes, the streets. At best, the style varies, but overall you're producing the same old song. The funny thing is, my favourite artists of the time stayed firmly within these subject boundaries and, on a purely musical level, I was more than satisfied. If there was a higher level of consciousness waiting to be unlocked, I didn't know how it would sound and, like the rest of the world, I was having a good enough time at this level to not care. Bear in mind, this was a monumental era for Black British music. In February, Stormzy's first album, *Gang Signs & Prayer* had reached number one in the UK Albums Chart and, after years of classic mixtapes, Nines hit number four with *One Foot Out*.

Stormzy and I entered the industry around the same time, while Nines grew up ten minutes down the road from me. All of us crossed paths every now and then, celebrated each other's work on social media and had overlapping circles. But even if I didn't feel these personal connections to them in particular, I was happy for UK Rap in general. Growing up we didn't think it was possible to go mainstream without losing that sauce, that thing that made Black listeners *feel* something and elevate the artist in the first place. The British music industry had a way of compromising our stars, watering down their material and buying them off with bigger (Whiter) audiences who rewarded these compromises. But Stormzy and Nines both struck a balance on their albums that didn't leave our scene feeling abandoned, allowing us to enjoy their success as genuine wins for the culture we had nurtured all these years. In May 2017, J Hus's debut album, *Common Sense*, charted at number six, and was eventually crowned 'album of the year' by *Complex* magazine. In my opinion, compared to Stormzy and Nines, Hus's rise signalled a slightly different cultural shift. To me, his music represented a new generation of Africans in Britain, who were mixing sounds and dialects to create something separate from Rap: Afro-Swing.

Vibrations

On Episode 26 of *Have You Heard George's Podcast?* (titled 'Vibrations'), I shared one of the biggest realisations of my life:

> Over thousands of miles of migration, Black people
> Stayed in sync through sounds and vibrations

I used that episode to sketch the similarities between US Hip Hop and Jamaican Dancehall. Pointing out the parallels in their origin, sound and content allowed me to explain my theory that this music was a medium of communication. It enabled parts of the impoverished Black diaspora to broadcast their perspective in their own language, creating a musical/mental space for reflection. This realisation fully dawned on me in 2017, with the explosion of Afro-Swing. To really understand this genre, you need to look at a few strands of Black British music between 2009 and 2014.

In the first half of this book, I laid out the decline of Grime music in the late 2010s, and how it influenced me to turn to poetry. This era saw the emergence of 'Road' Rap – which was grittier and more reality-based than Grime – but it also witnessed the rapid rise and fall of 'UK Funky'. Funky was like the opposite of Grime and Road Rap in terms of its content; it was all about parties and vibes. Like Grime, it generally stuck to a particular tempo, but placed a lot less emphasis on lyricism. The shift from content-driven, lyrical music to dance music turned out to be a key component in the development of Afro-Swing. The change was multifaceted; in a lot of this Black British music, you can hear different cultural elements. For example, UK Funky contained a strain of 1980s Chicago House music in its use of electronic instrumentation and 'four-to-the-floor' beats. Acts like CrazyCousinz and Ill Blu reminded me of this heritage. They produced some of my favourite UK Funky music, which was always made ten times better by female vocalists like Kyla, Shani Cuppcake, Meleka, Shystie, Princess Nyah, Bucie and Kimona. But Funky also had African and Caribbean influences, which acts like Donae'o and Fr3e incorporated beautifully. Over time, these African influences became more pronounced – another crucial part of Afro-Swing's conception. As my generation approached our twenties, we embraced the dance/vibes element of this new sound, which replaced the colder, more poker-faced energy of Grime and Rap. It was like we were rejecting what Britain made us, and returning to the motherland, sonically. Rappers didn't dance, but dance is an African language, which is why, in my opinion, the centre of US Hip Hop shifted over the 2000s from the East Coast (where rappers were reserved and stand-offish, like we used to be) to the Southern states, where rappers danced all the time. Anyway, the African strain of UK Funky was the longest-lasting element of the genre, surviving the wave of novelty dances that followed Gracious Kay's 'Migraine Skank', K.I.G.'s 'Head, Shoulders, Knees and Toes', Tribal Magz's 'Tribal Man Skank' and more. That trend started to annoy people after a while but, honestly, I loved all of it. I still think the actual music was underrated because the older crowd were put off by seeing their little brothers and sisters in colourful clothes jumping around in the club. Regardless, as we formed our own network of self-run club nights, acts like Mista Silva and Kwamz leaned more and more into the African elements – filling whole songs with chants that kept everyone dancing.

But even though Funky dominated the club, Rap wasn't over; it was just getting started. In Brixton, one of London's most iconic neighbourhoods, a young British Nigerian rapper called Sneakbo had an idea. In 2010, he rapped over Vybz Kartel's 'Touch a Button', creating a fusion of Road Rap and Jamaican Dancehall. Not since Giggs released 'Talkin' Da Hardest' in 2007 had there been such a craze over a UK Rap song. I remember being a youth worker on a summer programme in 2010, where all the kids, aged between eight and twelve, knew the words to Sneakbo's 'Touch Ah Button'. Following this innovation, more Rap/Dancehall crossovers came in the form of 'Every Gyal' by Chip featuring Mavado, and 'Messiah', a remix by Ratlin of another Mavado song. These are just two of the biggest examples, but Sneakbo and others carried this wave for a few years. This period was exciting for me because (as some of you will know from Episode 22 of *Have You Heard George's Podcast?*) I loved Dancehall – especially that Mavado/Vybz Kartel era. The music caught me just as I was becoming a rapper, but a few early experiments showed me that merging our UK sound with their Jamaican sound wouldn't be easy. In Jamaica, they played with melody in ways that our straitjacketed British culture didn't cultivate. I thought Jamaicans would find us unimaginative and one-dimensional, since our rappers only rapped, while their rappers sang, danced *and* rapped (way better than us, in my opinion). So, to see Mavado and Vybz both embracing our music, without our artists losing themselves in the process – that, for me, was priceless.

Meanwhile, African music was continuing to make its mark on Britain. Fuse ODG represented the earliest signs of a new, UK version of Afrobeats. His name was 'Fuse' for a reason; hits like 'Antenna' and 'Azonto' fused our Black British sound with Ghanaian dance energy and didn't fit into any particular box. In 2013, he smacked up the UK charts, reaching number five with 'Million Pound Girl', number seven with 'Antenna' and number thirty with 'Azonto'. This was unheard of, especially given that prior to 2013 Fuse was literally unheard of. His meteoric rise wasn't linked to a clever marketing campaign; he was embraced purely on the strength of his music. To many of us, this was an indication that things were changing. The following year, Timbo and Mover dropped 'Ringtone', which DJ Kenny Allstar once described as 'the door to the bridge of Afro-Rap and the evolution of Afro-Swing'. This song, in many ways, defined the coming era. Like Sneakbo's 'Touch Ah Button', it featured gangsta lyrics over an instrumental from an already popular song, but Mover's swagger combined with Timbo's melodies made it something new. Although Sneakbo was Nigerian, 'Ringtone' was much more African than his breakout hit in its references – the chorus contained the line 'fine boy, no pimple,' a flip from Wizkid's 2010 hit, 'Tease Me'.

Speaking of Wizkid, I can't talk about the rise of Afro-Swing without touching on the rise of Afrobeats. When I was a kid, Congolese music dominated African parties. This made sense, given the pioneering history of Congolese artists, dating back to their adaptation of Cuban *Son* in the 1930s. But by the 2010s, Nigerian and Ghanaian music had flooded the British African scene. I believe this is in part due to the make-up of our diaspora: Nigeria and Ghana are two of the biggest nationalities in Black Britain. But the ascension of their music is also owed to years of hard work, which culminated in the crossover success of the D'Banj/Don Jazzy/P Square generation. This success was carried over by the Wizkid/Burna Boy/Davido generation and has grown exponentially ever since. I love this story because, as you can see from their early videos, these guys built their platform from the ground up. In an unbelievably short time, they closed the commercial and aesthetic distance between their early music scene and not just ours in the UK, but that of the biggest in the world: America.

You might have noticed that music from West Africa features more prominently in this story than sounds from the East. As I mentioned, my theory is that the ethnic composition of Black Britain dictates the dominant influences of our genres. For example, when I was growing up, the Jamaican diaspora was the biggest contingent in Black London. Yet, over the course of my lifetime, increased immigration from West Africa tipped the scales, and by the time I was twenty, Nigerians and Ghanaians outnumbered Jamaicans. This was reflected in the switch from Dancehall to Afrobeats as the main sound of the Black club scene, which I witnessed from my teens to my twenties. However, it's hard to pin down how music works. We don't have a lot of

African Americans over here, but we always listen to their songs. You could say that's because they've had the most influential industry for the longest, which I did actually argue on Episode 21 of *Have You Heard George's Podcast*, 'Flying the Flag'. Yet British teenagers nowadays are listening to more UK Rap than ever – is this because there are more UK rappers than before? Is it because of the groundwork I outlined above? What about modern Congolese music? For some reason, despite it still enjoying audiences of millions around the world, the Congolese scene has faded from British African party life significantly since the nineties. How do you examine the reasons why? My life experience tells me that certain circumstances cause people to listen to their local sounds more or less at different points in their lives. But it's hard to tell if listening to local sounds more necessarily means rejecting external sounds as well.

Uganda is a confusing example. The Ugandan music scene, like every other Black music scene, has grown so much over the last twenty years. Pioneers like Bobi Wine, Juliana Kanyomozi, Bebe Cool, Judith Babirye and Mesach Semakula are now able to enjoy lucrative careers, but it was different when they started in the early 2000s. Back then, like the Grime legends of my teens, they were just lighting the spark to carry the torch for an overlooked music market. These guys paved the way for later sensations like Radio & Weasel, Navio, Rabadaba and Grace Nakimera, who took the torch and led the Ugandan scene to new heights. Following this generation came that of Rema Namakula, Sheebah, Eddy Kenzo, Winnie Nwagi, Spice Diana and Fik Fameica. They all worked exceptionally hard to overcome Uganda's infrastructural challenges and keep audiences entertained in an age of relentless competition. By this point, their videos had reached international standards (at the same rate as more famous West Africans) and they offered a range of

Ugandan sounds – from Rema's more traditional, sweet-girl vibe to Fik's high-energy ghetto-boy music. But here's the thing: while the Ugandan music scene has gone from strength to strength, the popularity of Nigerian music in Uganda has also grown – a lot. So, in this case, more local consumption doesn't mean less international consumption.

But it gets deeper. Local consumption can vary across a big enough country, and over time this might change how much local listeners care about music from other regions. Take US Hip Hop; early on, everyone listened to New York rappers, until places like California, Florida, Texas and New Orleans produced their own stars, who often meant more to their local audiences. As a result, the past twenty years has seen subgenres of Hip Hop spring up in different parts of America – from Trap in Atlanta to Drill in Chicago. How has this affected New York Hip Hop? In 2021, the South accounted for 55 per cent of US Hip Hop streams, compared to the East Coast's 16 per cent, according to Spotify. But what about the West Coast? After dominating the charts in the early nineties with the invention of Gangsta Rap, the West Coast only accounted for 4 per cent of Hip Hop streams in 2021. I don't have the numbers for the British scene, but I have the memories. Back in the day, UK Rap was almost synonymous with London. But over the years, Birmingham, Manchester and Liverpool have all produced national stars. In America's case, more localised subgenres seem to correlate with less interest in the original home of Hip Hop. I don't know if this is the same over here, though. In fact, as someone who was part of the first Grime wave, I remember when it was a niche genre. Some of the middle-class White and Asian boys in my school found it comical, while others got it, and wanted to be part of it. I'm not a teenager anymore, and I haven't done enough formal research on this, but I feel like today's UK Rap scene is almost undisputed among that demographic, regardless of cultural background. I'll get back to you on that – just wait for my PhD.

So, what dictates the popularity of local music? My guess would be a sustained period of improvements in production and distribution (i.e. personalised internet access, affordable equipment, streaming platforms), as well as a constant flow of locally produced music that is also locally embraced. In the case of Grime, Road Rap, UK Funky and Afro-Swing, all these factors played an important role. I already told you about my friend, Rashid Kasirye, another Ugandan from my neighbourhood. I was chilling in his flat when he first told me about his new online platform, Link Up TV. I think it was around 2009. That platform ended up being key to the rise of Afro-Swing, launching classics like 'Messiah' by Ratlin and 'Ringtone' by Timbo and Mover, both of which we looked at earlier. I find it crazy how so much of UK music has come to be represented by people I grew up around, but it's less crazy when you understand my local scene. In the same way, East London gave birth to Grime, so it's no surprise that it also produced the scene's leading online channel, GRM Daily. In 2014, GRM released a freestyle by an unknown young rapper called J Hus. His unconventional style caught everyone's attention and before long, Hus released a mixtape, *The 15th Day*. This landmark effort was my favourite thing in UK music for a while, and featured production from a team called JOAT. They were all talented producers, but one member stood out in particular. His name was Jae5 (pronounced 'Jay Five') and, before long, he would become the undisputed king of Afro-Swing. Jae5's two younger brothers, Kruddz and ODG, were in a group called NSG. The crew have joked over the years about what these letters stand for, but my favourite explanation is 'Nigeria-Slash-Ghana', reflecting the fact that three of NSG's members are Nigerian and three are Ghanaian. Since 2018, NSG have been on an incredible run, releasing hit after hit and touring the world. I think they might be the first British act in our generation to tour Africa. My cousin, John 'Mase' Masembe, handled the tour in August 2022. I'm still pissed that I missed it.

The Afro-Swing sound was evolved even further by Yxng Bane (pronounced 'Young Bane') and Kojo Funds, who came through a little later. In August 2016, the two collaborated on Bane's song 'Fine Wine', released on Link Up TV. By this point, it was clear that something new had fully taken shape, but there was no name for it. A follower of the Black British music scene would notice the influence of UK Funky in the song's light-hearted, uncomplicated, flirtatious content. But at the same time, everything about the 'Fine Wine' video said 'Road' – as in, this came from Road Rap. The whole visual features a bunch of serious-looking guys in a penthouse with some pretty women. It's hard to explain how strange this would have looked just five years earlier; street guys weren't singing sweet songs back then. Maybe to balance it out, Kojo followed up with his hit 'Dun Talkin''. This time he combined the same melodic vibe with grittier lyrics but, trust me, whatever he said didn't make a difference – the song became a party anthem. How do I know? A few months after its release I was a groomsman at the wedding of my close friends, Nathan and Natalie, and 'Dun Talkin'' was the soundtrack we all stepped out to. Kojo Funds is actually credited as the one who coined the term 'Afro-Swing', finally giving a name to a genre that launched the careers of many more, such as MoStack, a friend of J Hus, and Not3s (pronounced 'Notes'). Fun fact – Not3s was actually one of the kids at that summer programme I worked on back in 2010. In just a few years, I saw him grow from a cheeky twelve-year-old to an international star with hits like 'Aladdin' and 'Addison Lee'. J Hus, JOAT, Jae5,

NSG, Yxng Bane, Kojo Funds, Not3s – all East Londoners, all West Africans. This is what I meant when I said:

> Over thousands of miles of migration, Black people
> Stayed in sync through sounds and vibrations

Although the Afro-Swing scene has contracted a bit since its peak in 2017, the careers of its biggest stars are still going stronger than ever. It was this genre that opened my eyes to the unique role music plays in creating space for young Black people to reinterpret the world. That might sound like an overstatement, but only if you take the music at face value. It's easy to roll your eyes at a cheesy line or to dismiss a song as nothing more than 'catchy', but when the same marginalised minorities from some of the most volatile parts of the country consistently blend and reimagine sounds in a way that captures the world's attention, there's clearly something going on that needs to be understood.

18

From Poetry to Podcasting

So, why cram all of this into a book that started off as an autobiography? Because once I broke away from the music industry – which I joined after a long period of institutionalisation in the British education system – this was the reality my eyes slowly opened up to. Poetry for me has always been the pursuit of truth. A line comes together in my mind when I see a situation clearly and, by 2017, all my lines about Black life were turning stale. I could hear myself constantly going over the same questions and coming up with the same answers.

> Question: *Why are we, as Black people, so disconnected from each other?*
>
> Answer: *Because we live in a world that sees our unity as a threat.*
>
> Question: *How do we, as Black people, move forward?*
>
> Answer: *Get money and organise our communities.*

My understanding was general, superficial and vague. After all those years of 'elite' education, I didn't have a clue what was really going on with Black people – with Africa. Part of the reason I took my nephews to Uganda that year was because I felt alienated from African truth in Britain. I watched Al Jazeera daily and followed Ugandan news where I could, but my basic orientation was Western. My social media feed, my consumption patterns, my whole lifestyle set me up to think in ways that were completely detached from Africa . . . and that made me uncomfortable. I didn't want to end up like Obama – drawing authority from an anti-Black power structure. I also didn't want to fall into anti-Blackness through my work, which often happens to Black artists in Western industries. With all of this on my mind, a new character walked into my imagination one day. Her name was Sanyu, and she was born to resolve the creative tensions in my mind.

New Rules

Spending my whole summer with a seven-year-old and a five-year-old opened me up in unexpected ways. Throughout our Ugandan adventures, I ended up watching a lot of kiddies' movies, listening to loads of primary-school banter and re-learning the world through my nephews' eyes. Our earlier trip to Disneyworld gave me an appreciation of their favourite animated films, so I'd happily sit through endless replays of *Despicable Me* and *Hotel Transylvania*. The joy on my nephews' faces reminded me of that magical time in my own life when movies and cartoons had the same effect on me. In animation, the characters were constantly shapeshifting to exaggerate familiar emotions, while the settings were so creative they made me feel like I was in a different world. I remembered how *Dexter's Laboratory* stretched my ideas about what could be hidden in the walls of a house, and how *The Lion King's* elephant graveyard made a skeleton look like a giant playground. Every night in Uganda, after I put the boys to bed, I would re-watch their favourite scenes, studying them like works of art and science. What drew me to animation was the unrestricted possibilities it carried; I wanted the same for my poetry.

Since my earliest days as a rapper, I resented the rules. These rules – which we learned from mainstream Rap – told us what 'success' looked like, and therefore how we should act. If you didn't follow the rules, you wouldn't fit the pattern, and if you didn't fit the pattern, you couldn't make it as a rapper. Most rules change – some slower than others – but generally, ever since Gangsta Rap blew up in the 1990s, the rules have stayed obedient to capital and indifferent to Black life. For example, before its commercial take-off, US Hip Hop was driven by youthful creativity that celebrated all sorts of personalities, from KRS One's street scholar to Queen Latifah's soul sister. Since the nineties, however, the most consistent character types in mainstream Rap have been the violent criminal and the sex machine. Unlike the militancy and liberation politics of previous generations, chart-topping Hip Hop portrays violence and sex in ways that make a lot of money and contradict or ignore the Black struggle. In other words, mainstream Rap depicts Black life in ways that support the power structure, rather than challenge it – and this is what I resented as a young rapper.

From the music we consumed to the dynamics of our area, it was like we were constantly being groomed to become more selfish and more disconnected every day. For this reason, I used my writing to create my own rules. I straight-up ignored the pressure to conform, and tried to earn a reputation off the strength of rhymes that portrayed my world as creatively as possible. In terms of audience-building, it was an uphill struggle all the way. Almost no one in my age group wanted to hear 'conscious' lyrics like mine, but I couldn't deny my reality. The thought of switching to spoken word came after four years of this, and it made everything click; street poetry was an easier sell than conscious Rap. I had found a way to be heard without breaking my own rules, and it all came down to *framing*. By framing my rhymes as poems, I offered listeners something different enough to stand out, but familiar enough to fit in. Years on, my experience in the music industry made it clear that I needed a new approach, which is why in the summer of 2017, I started taking a closer look at animation.

Sanyu

In July of that year, I had arrived in Uganda with just my nephews and our luggage, but the following month I left with much more. A few weeks before our return to the UK, my own animated character had walked into my thoughts during a trip to Gayaza High School for Girls, where I was sent on an errand by my mum. While there, I took in the playful voices around me, and marvelled at one of the school's most innovative projects. It was called 'Farm Camp' – a farm where students studied agriculture, on the basis that this was still the backbone of Uganda's economy. Their homework in other subjects was made relevant to the farm in order to give context to what they were learning. I had never seen a project like this but I liked it. I just wished there was a way to make the learning even more accessible; a way of stepping into the mind of a Gayaza girl and walking through her Farm Camp experience. Wouldn't that open the project up to the millions of Ugandan children who didn't go to Gayaza? Wouldn't this set a new standard of *edutainment*? Wouldn't it make a great animation?

Her name was Sanyu, one of my favourite Ugandan names, meaning 'joy'. All the Sanyus I've known have been smiley, happy-go-lucky people, as many Ugandans are, so her character was clear from the beginning. This little voice in my head represented the Gayaza girl who could talk Ugandan children through what she was learning at school – like a cute little study buddy. The problem was, I knew nothing about being a Gayaza girl. So, after visiting the school, I parked the idea and returned to London. But over the next few weeks, a strange emotion started rising in my chest. After spending the previous two years of post-record-label independence testing different ideas (but not committing to any), I felt guilty for neglecting this one in particular. Sanyu's character was so clear in my mind that I could visualise her clearly, and – as weird as this sounds – I could sense her fear. She felt like the walls were closing in, and her claustrophobia was justified. My mind can be a crowded place, so the anxiety felt by this little Gayaza girl in such a chaotic environment made complete sense to me. Day and night, Sanyu would plead with me not to forget her, latching on to my thoughts, trying to prove her relevance to my future. For the first time in my life, I was able to see the inside of my head from the perspective of one of my many ideas. Something told me this alone was a breakthrough worth writing about . . . so I wrote.

Since I saw Sanyu as an animated character, I used music from one of my favourite animated films to find her voice. This was Disney's 1991 classic, *Beauty and the Beast* – I found the whole score online and, for about a week, listened to it on repeat, trying to come up with Sanyu's first words. Eventually I moved on to other non-animated classics from my childhood, like *Jurassic Park* and *The Nutty Professor*. These films transported me to my childhood, which I valued because of my nephews' influence on me that year. But Sanyu's voice didn't become clear in my mind until I finally landed on the soundtrack of *Matilda*. This 1996 release was a film adaptation of Roald Dahl's book of the same name. Being about a little girl with magic powers, the movie had music that fitted Sanyu's journey perfectly. Now I had no excuse – this idea was going to come out one way or another. So, I completely abandoned all other music and locked myself in my room, writing and recording about three short stories introducing the character of Sanyu over music from *Matilda*. On these demos, I performed Sanyu's lines in a Ugandan accent, which I then pitched up on my laptop, creating a whole new voice that sounded nothing like me, and a lot like a young Gayaza girl. This was the most creative I had been in a long time. Months of unconscious re-education by my nephews started playing out in this new undefined project. It's like I had absorbed their go-with-the-flow nature, as well as their tendency to imagine wild, impossible things. Under their influence, the writer in me had evolved into a new kind of storyteller. These early Sanyu demos were more like short cartoons for your ears than actual poems. Like the characters in my nephews' favourite movies, Sanyu's lines were funny and the world she described was endlessly imaginative. Finally, after two years in the creative wilderness, I was back.

A Newfound Urgency

While I was away with the fairies, chasing my inner thoughts, the world was still spinning, and some days it felt like it was spinning out of control.

In November 2017, footage emerged of Black Africans being sold on open-air slave markets in Libya. Cries of anger from around the world were intense, but short-lived. Before long the news cycle moved on and the international community's limited response was almost forgotten. The whole thing prompted me to look more seriously at the so-called 'migrant crisis' that had been in the headlines for years, as many of the Africans detained in Libya were only passing through the country to reach Europe. I learned that since the assassination of former Libyan leader Muammar Gaddafi, Libya had become what many described as a 'failed state', with different parts of the country controlled by competing militias. I also learned that the EU was doing everything it could to avoid the real issues driving irregular migration – conflict and poverty, largely fuelled by Western powers. Instead of uniting against violence and slave labour in the Democratic Republic of Congo or ending the French exploitation of Central and West Africa, Europe was reframing the migrant crisis as an isolated issue of 'human trafficking'. This rhetoric hid the fact that migrants often paid smugglers to help them migrate illegally out of pure desperation. Racist and classist borders were the main reason for this. It is much easier for a European to enter an African country and extract wealth than it is for an African to enter Europe and get a low-paying job. A focus on human trafficking allowed the EU to militarise its handling of the crisis, pretending to set migrants free from evil traffickers by paying African governments (and sometimes traffickers themselves) to capture and return migrants to their place of origin.

Sanyu, my latest creation, had evolved faster than I could have imagined, but now I was being pulled in another direction. Her first purpose was to become an animated tutor, yet just a few months of development had transformed her into a genuinely original concept: an idea with a voice. Through her mission to make it out of my head into the real world, Sanyu could appeal to infants, educators, entrepreneurs – *anyone*.

The options were limitless. In fact, by this point I was sure that I could take Sanyu far before turning to animation, which seemed expensive and inaccessible to me. It made much more sense to continue creating short stories about her time in my head, since I had finally found the right vehicle for these stories: a podcast.

Podcasting

My teenage obsession with changing the rules of Rap had paid off over the years. As a poet, I learned how to write more of myself into my rhymes, and how to rhyme without a beat. As a recording artist, I learned how to blend genres and tell complex stories. Now, as an independent creator, I was more ambitious. Sanyu's potential was bigger than anything I'd ever attempted; she could *teach* and, in order to do so, she needed more space than the average song or poem. First, I planned to make an album out of her adventures. I still contemplate this, and believe it would work, but at the time I decided an album would leave me too boxed-in. Beyond Sanyu, I craved the freedom to talk about any- and everything, which would make an album too disjointed. And anyway, my journey had taught me the value of having something different – in 2017, that could only be a podcast.

19

The Bigger Picture

By telling my story, I've laid out my predicament: I'm a Black entertainer on the frontline of the War on Blackness, but it's not always clear who I'm fighting for; is it the children of Africa or their abusers? Through my poetry, I've shone a light on many aspects of Black life, which I do in solidarity with Afro-descended people everywhere, but this poetry has been funded and distributed by a media industry that platforms endless strategies of anti-Blackness. Yes, my listeners say I've inspired them over the years, but I've only ever done so without critiquing capitalism – i.e. dealing with the symptoms, not the sickness. Does this mean I accept the inequality that the system creates?

I've come to the disappointing realisation that I'm useful to Western media for all the wrong reasons. As a 'good' immigrant who went to school, stayed out of trouble and rose to fame with non-threatening poems that criticised my own community for the problems it faced, I presented a narrative that aligned with ruling-class interests. I made the system look good. All those people claiming that racism and poverty were holding them back just needed to be more like me – to work hard and expect no favours (as if poverty doesn't force you to do that anyway). OK, I'm being a little unfair to myself. My poetry has always dealt with the injustices imposed on my people and, to be fair, in the early days I was writing to oppose the weird anti-Black themes of mainstream Rap, but my overall thing was 'let's work within the system to change what we can'. This message came from a deep commitment to self-reliance, which, now that I think about it, came from insecurities about my neighbourhood and our relationship with the government. These insecurities bled into my art, driving me to push back against mainstream Rap's weirdness. However, without a radical analysis of society, I could only push back by promoting self-help to my corner of the ghettoised Black diaspora (like a real liberal cliché). And in my efforts to do so, I wrote poems that talked to my listeners on a *personal* level – saying, '*Close your eyes and feel my pain,*' instead of '*Statistics show . . .*' But as a child of the 1990s immersed in the Western mainstream, I couldn't help painting an individualistic, pro-capitalist picture of social change, repeating mistakes made by Booker T. Washington a hundred years prior. It's not that my poetry said '*Stop complaining, get money,*' it's more that I had no concept of collective struggle or real political education. Looking back, it feels like I spent as much time denouncing the effects of poverty as I did breaking down the causes. That's not a good ratio.

Black Conservatism

I guess I'm describing the process of becoming a Black conservative. It's a trap you fall into once you accept the brazenness of the West, and become attached to whatever perks it has to offer. To conserve means to keep something as it is and, for Black people, this is a complex instinct. We may want to conserve our family values, or our cultural distinctions from overbearing Western trends. And the way we do this sometimes appears to be through hard-won access to institutions that our ancestors fought for us to enter. Yet, as centuries of evidence suggests, none of this promises the change we need.

In my case, formal education hid the racist world order from me, while also giving me a route out of the low-income, marginalised status of my community. It never occurred to me that this status was manufactured, like the educational prestige I was betting my future on. So, by extension, it never occurred to me that the majority of my peers would never access the same opportunities as me. Therefore, it also never occurred to me that the global economy was designed to work this way. This oversight prevents a lot of well-off Black people from engaging with the reality faced by most people of African descent. The time many Black conservatives spend working in White spaces takes them away from Black life, filling their heads with perspectives that affirm the status quo, and distorting their view of Black issues.

To the untrained eye, I didn't look like this kind of conservative, but by focusing on the symptoms of poverty, and not the causes, while pursuing an education outside of my community that didn't deal with our history, I was becoming insensitive to those who had a much harder life than me. This conservative strain in my thinking was reinforced when I became George the Poet, as I now enjoyed a growing audience that liked what I had to say. It started with Black students and rappers who saw me as a breath of fresh air, and extended to non-Black audiences of all ages, which complicated things, although it's what I wanted. This hybrid audience gave me a career based on my ability to make them *feel* something – not to facilitate real change. That's not a criticism of my audience; I'm truly thankful for every listener, journalist, blogger or DJ who has appreciated and shared my work. It means a lot to me that in an imperfect world with our imperfect selves, we've connected meaningfully over something I put my best intentions into. The problem is, when my self-help ethos is turned into a message directed at a whole class of poor, racialised people, in full view of everyone else, it can be used to suggest that the solution to inequality is more personal responsibility from marginalised people – not a change of system. This myth is promoted by the individualism at the heart of celebrity culture in general, but mainstream Rap in particular. It shapes the values and dreams of our children, while completely downplaying the scale of organised violence Black people have faced all along.

Structural Injustice vs Personal Responsibility

In reality, society benefits from its members having both an understanding of structural injustice and a sense of personal responsibility. But corporate media make it seem like these two principles are at war – as if people should only expect decency from themselves, not their employers, their politicians or the systems that rule their lives. When public-sector workers go on strike for better pay, powerful news outlets and wealthy pundits accuse them of punishing society with their selfish, bratty demands. I hate this distortion of reality on behalf of all working people, but it really bothers me to see Black people being roped into such bad-faith arguments. We have bigger problems than the fight for a better deal within the rich countries we've ended up in (although this fight is necessary). The wealth of these societies is rooted in the ongoing dehumanisation of Africans in general. That dehumanisation has denied Africans many of the protections afforded to Europeans, and the West's unwillingness to admit this makes it hard for the Black diaspora to develop a political platform that will put an end to our vulnerability. Think of anything bad – war, unclean water, precarious work, natural disasters – White populations have layers of protection from these things that have been constructed at the expense of darker peoples. If we don't normalise this economic understanding across the diaspora and the West overall, we'll have to keep discussing inequality in ways that miss the point, and we'll never build the momentum we need. For this reason, it really is crucial that we don't waste all our energy on relatively minor, individualistic battles that have limited global relevance, and only serve to make our oppression more comfortable.

Active Learning

By my late twenties, a lifetime of propaganda had restricted my imagination so effectively that I couldn't really critique capitalism without the help of a lot of books – ones that the mainstream didn't promote. From classics like Kwame Nkrumah's *Neo-Colonialism* to modern essentials like Mehrsa Baradaran's *The Color of Money*, I found crystal-clear explanations of how the world really works in literature that neither school nor TV would ever present to me.[30] Growing up in St Raph's, we used to watch older guys pull up to the block and hand out boxes of fresh Nikes to whoever was around, then chill in their cars playing loud music and counting street money. To me, *that* was capitalism: a cycle of getting paid and getting things. I didn't know about the debt and violence that underpinned the production of money. I saw the flow of finance as a part of nature that favoured some over others, like good weather or fresh water. Before the books, I learned from my surroundings, slowly pushing for deeper understanding as I went on. That shift from passive to active learning helped me break out of the mainstream echo chambers that filtered the views I had access to. But I continued to study my surroundings, using music to do so. And over time, a deeper understanding of music's role in Black life led me to study exploitation, which changed everything. I learned that Black music, like the resources of Africa, Asia, Latin America, the Caribbean and Australasia, was controlled and exploited by capitalists. I learned that this class of owners had perfected the art of telling stories that justify why their power over everyone else is fair. And I realised that Black music, like all art under capitalism, is used to support those stories.

Valuing Value

Black music comes from the bodies of Black artists. It is proof that value does not start with wealth. And as we learned from our years as struggling rappers, it also proves that value can be cultivated without wealth. So why do we sign this value away to record labels? Because capitalism likes zero-sum competition: in order for someone to win, someone else must lose. In this case, the competition for ownership of Black music is dominated by Western capitalists, because whatever wealth we have as Black people cannot compete with the wealth of Western industry. By opening ourselves up to Western capital and using the physical, legal and financial infrastructure that comes with it, we feed our value into the world market the same way our home countries do cheap labour and natural resources: via the capitalists of Western Europe and North America. It's a colonial dynamic that offers no chance for Black people to control the mass distribution of their art on a scale that reflects the experience that creates it. At the start of my journey, I did not know I would discover this. Naively, I had accepted propaganda that tells us capitalism is democratic. I genuinely believed that the defining factor of success in this system is work ethic. And for all its problems, Grime seemed to prove this to me.

I wasn't surprised when the genre gained a new level of commercial success and international recognition in the mid-2010s, a decade after we tried to make it work, because some of the most creative, committed and talented people eventually became Grime's biggest names. It seemed fair. But was it? The vast majority of MCs didn't make it, despite years of hard work. And for those who did, success has been measured by access to the White capital that once ignored them and continues to ignore their communities. This is how politically uneducated rappers end up being useless, if not counterproductive, to their places of origin. They distract young listeners from systemic analysis while glorifying inequality and posing as allies of the poor. But it would be disingenuous of me to pretend that this is just a Rap problem. In general, (Black) celebrities have yet to form a class that is of any material value to the (Black) masses. They live and vote according to no other agenda than their tax bracket.

Get Up, Stand Up

I finished *Track Record* during the most surreal time of my life: Sandra and I were in the final days of expecting our firstborn. My wife had endured the entire pregnancy – and really, our whole relationship – with this book hovering over us, and I was relieved to be completing it just as our son arrived. Watching Sandra become the mother of my child was like being born again myself. Our centre of gravity shifted, and there was no space inside me for anything other than total devotion to our family. But sometimes, when I think about the world Sandra and I have created together, it doesn't take long for my mind to drift to the world we'll leave behind for our boy. There is no right way of preparing a Black child for reality, but it's a task that can't be ignored. In the months before my little brother Michael was born, I remember wondering who he would be and what questions he would ask me. Twenty-six years later, those thoughts came back in the run up to meeting our newborn son. I don't know what he'll ask me, but I know what I want to tell him.

I want to tell my son that things are getting better; that all life is valued equally, new technology is solving old problems and no one is being left behind. I'd love to tell him that the world is a compassionate place, and that no amount of artificial intelligence could ever substitute what's inside him. I want to smile when I hear the songs of his generation, knowing that the happiness they bring isn't a distraction from the tragedies behind the music. But, as I've spent most of this book explaining, a lot needs to change before I can say any of that with confidence.

In reality, our ability to understand what's working and what's not is limited by the bad media diet that corporations force-feed us. And the sad truth is, these corporations use their money to turn Black music into a propaganda tool. By not dealing with the War on Blackness, the music gives the impression that things aren't so bad, because who has time to party in a crisis? Furthermore, the wealth acquired by commercially successful artists motivates them to avoid any collective struggle that might threaten their privilege. But this hasn't been a story about individual choice; it's about structural racism and class warfare. Wealth is the members' club of the ruling class.

Never in the history of capitalism has a Black person gained access to this club and changed the way it operates. To be real, the best Black wealth could do would be to finance the liberation struggle, and why would it do that? Colonialism gave strength to the Western currencies that wealth is earned in. So, what's going to happen to Western-backed Black wealth when Africa, Asia and Latin America finally break free from the need to trade in those currencies? This is what true liberation looks like, and it will require a level of humility from the West that the modern world has never seen.

Conclusion

Looking back on my life, I feel a mixture of pride and disappointment. I'm proud of my personal trajectory – studying, carving out my own path away from what was laid out for me, reaping the benefits of my commitment to creativity. But I can only feel disappointed with much of what that path has revealed. This disappointment stems from the answer to a question I've seen posed to many successful artists and entrepreneurs: what played a bigger part in your success – hard work or luck? Regardless of who is being asked, or how hard they've worked, I believe the only real answer is luck.

My journey has revealed to me that the majority of humanity is born into injustice; a world in which our ability to choose the life we want is shaped by where we live, and who our ancestors were. At the start of this journey, I had questions about the differences between the lives of my neighbourhood friends and my grammar-school friends. Sociology gave me some tools to think about this, but I would never find all the answers in formal education. Only through art was I able to put the pieces of the puzzle together. I studied the lyrics, production and distribution of my favourite music, while growing into my own as an artist. This process has always given me case studies of how the world works, inspiring me to make art that offers even more scope for study. So, from the outset of my career, I've tried effecting a shift in the narration of our lived experiences by showing others (first my friends, then my partners in the music industry) how to use the skills of our artistry to create critical analysis that's entertaining. My growing audience disproved all the tropes of people being uninterested in progressive messaging from Black artists. I'm proud of my work. With the help of people like my brothers, Michael and Kenny, my wife and manager, Sandra, my favourite collaborators, Benbrick, Miles and Jojo, plus so many more, this poetry has consistently uncovered new, unexplored corners of innovation that were quickly populated with younger artists inspired by my approach. People, essentially, proved me right. What stood in opposition to my belief in the potential of our music was . . . power.

Without a doubt, my experience in the music industry confirmed most of what I had read about the power dynamics of media production, or – for the social scientists out there – the political economy of art under capitalism. Within that system, I witnessed the suppression of my social analysis and the amplification of my non-challenging material. In real-time, I was taught that the role of mainstream music is to reproduce a certain image of the world, and my aspirations for young listeners clashed with that image. As I watched my soon-to-be award-winning work suffer delays and underfunding by my record label, it slowly dawned on me that they didn't care how commercially viable this work might be. At first, that struck me as an issue of laziness; not everyone wants to work outside their comfort zone, and I was presenting something unfamiliar. It blew my mind to think that a corporation would pass on a pioneering business model that could unlock an untapped market (since I was the only poet in the music industry) just because its employees were unmotivated to try something new. And although that's definitely a thing that happens in corporations, nowadays I see my industry experience a bit differently. I believe the real issue was one of conflicting intentions. The artistic analysis I offered was the ideological opposite of Western 'popular' music. The most visible, corporate-backed rappers don't challenge the status quo. They don't show any angst about selling the same broken image of their communities over and over again. In fact, as wealth has become the core obsession of Rap, the most visible rappers don't even acknowledge the existence of any community. This is an ideological preference of the corporate overlords funding mainstream music. It's clear to me now that I was playing a losing game. I was asking too many questions, stepping on too many toes and operating in the wrong space for real social enquiry. I don't believe everyone at the label thought this – capitalist ideology disguises itself in clever ways – but it was widely understood in my community. Those on the sharp end of structural injustice are generally better poised to recognise systemic sabotage than those who are raised to trust the system.

Funnily enough, that's not all I learned about power. Although my career can be read as a series of achievements against the odds, I did enjoy privileges that set me apart. My grammar-school experience prepared me for a life of code-switching, which influenced my pivot from Rap to Spoken Word. This was a differentiating factor that separated me from all the rappers I grew up with, some of whom were undeniably better than me, but couldn't overcome the problems of our area. To take it even further back, getting into Queen Elizabeth's School could be attributed to my own mother's privileged upbringing in Uganda. She wanted me to go to the British equivalent of Gayaza High School for Girls, a top-performing, colonial-era institution known for academic excellence. In fact, both my parents attended reputable schools that gave them a Western education and a strong grasp of the English language – imperial privileges that didn't reach the masses of newly impoverished Ugandans in their generation. This enabled them to guide me all the way to the University of Cambridge, an institution that compounded these intergenerational privileges in my life. In my last year of Cambridge I studied two modules that, in many ways, informed my career: 'The Political Economy of Capitalism' and 'Media, Culture and Society'. Much of what you've read in this book has been shaped by the analytical frameworks I got from those modules – privileges that many young artists don't have. I entered my record deal knowing that ownership of mass media was becoming increasingly concentrated in the hands of a few. I'd had time to process what this meant for us as artists, and how this trend reflected the broader drift of capitalism towards global monopolies, so my eventual decision to leave the industry for the independent route wasn't a hard one. Owing to all these privileges, I never felt boxed in. Yes, I worked hard, but I was lucky to have been given opportunities to think critically and respond creatively in the first place.

A recent trip to Uganda drove home how lucky I have been, as it always does. I apologise for sounding like a patronising cliché here; poverty in Uganda continues to devastate a huge segment of the population, and many Ugandans are understandably sensitive about discussing this in non-African spaces. And although I'm rattled whenever I see the humiliation that homeless Ugandans experience, or the day-to-day struggles of Kampala's working class (as documented in Episode 38 of my podcast, 'Once Upon a Time in Kampala'), this recent trip opened my eyes to something else. After my wife and I made the impromptu decision to put on a show for my Ugandan audience, I sat down for an interview with Kampala rapper, Wonder JR, arranged by the venue we were using, MoTIV UG. Wonder was a tall, well-groomed and charismatic guy who gave the subtle impression that he came from wealth, mainly from his accent and unforced use of Black London slang – an indication of international exposure among a certain demographic. Wonder revealed that he'd been a long-time fan, which was humbling, given that he himself was a talented artist with a recent hit song that made him a bona fide celebrity in Uganda ('Parte Yani', a collaboration with pioneering Ugandan rapper Ruyonga and my good friend Zex Bilangilangi). After studying in the UK for some years, Wonder came home with a head full of inspiration from our Black British music scene, which he experienced during the era I explored earlier; the rise of Afro-Swing and the subsequent explosion of UK Drill. Wonder's dream was to uplift Ugandan creatives by bringing innovation to various industries, but, according to him, this was a non-starter. During our interview, the rapper expressed his frustration at being told 'this is not how we do things' by incumbents of those industries. He praised his mother for unexpectedly warming to his music career after initial doubts, but complained of feeling stifled by the resistance to change that was commonplace in Ugandan society. I'll never forget how he summarised his frustration: after living in the UK among young people who were forging their own path ahead, Wonder had returned to UG, where the constant message was 'slow down, fall in line'. He explained to me that *Have You Heard George's Podcast?* was like a window into a world of possibility, which to him represented a freedom of thought that was denied to even the most privileged Ugandans.

My conversation with Wonder JR was the inverse of so many conversations I've had with Ugandans about how lucky they were to be raised in Uganda. I've always criticised the imperial hangovers, the social coldness and the immortality of racism within British society, as a means of awakening Ugandans to their own privileges. I'm used to seeing that reflective look on the faces of my cousins and friends who had assumed that life in Europe was better than life in Africa, without knowing the reality of debt, loneliness and discrimination that pervades European life. But never before had the tables been turned on me. I had never been awakened to the privileges that were invisible to me, beyond the obvious advantages of proximity to White capital. It took a conversation with a well-off Ugandan to help me realise the psychological benefits I had enjoyed through my Western upbringing. This is not to overstate the case; I'm not suggesting that growing up in the West automatically makes you a lateral thinker. Instead I'm acknowledging that my specific experience granted me the space to think outside the box, and put those thoughts into action.

Still, as I emphasised earlier, there's a difference between my personal journey and the collective drift of humanity. Capitalism allows for a few like me and Wonder JR, with a random set of intersecting privileges, to break away from the path set out for the masses of working people from which we emerge. Stories like mine are elevated (instead of the widespread analysis I am pushing for) as a means of legitimising a system that intentionally degrades human life. As I write, it has been announced that the UK has gone into recession, while energy provider British Gas has reported record profits of £751 million, up from £72 million the previous year – an increase of almost 1,000 per cent! It took me a day to accept that those were real numbers; I kept convincing myself I'd misread the figures, because my brain couldn't process my disgust. Levels of exploitation that were once saved for Black and Brown peoples in the global South are now normalised across the imperial North, but the bad news doesn't stop there.

The world has been further divided by Israel's most recent

assault on the Palestinian people of Gaza, following a military operation that claimed the lives of hundreds of people on 7 October 2023. This came seventy-five years after the majority of Gazans' ancestors were violently displaced from their homes in a purge known as the *Nakba* (Arabic for 'catastrophe'), in which Jews who had faced persecution in Europe drove Arab Palestinians out of their homes, following the Western-backed establishment of the Israeli state *on* the state of Palestine in 1947. Despite Israel admitting to firing indiscriminately at its own citizens during the 7 October attack; despite forty-two Israeli survivors suing Israeli security forces for not acting on prior knowledge of an impending military action; despite the majority of Gazans being women and children who had no involvement in the attack; despite Israel controlling Gazans' access to food, water, electricity and internet through a military blockade that has been in place for longer than 50 per cent of Gazans have been alive; despite Israeli politicians bragging about war crimes and being met with racist, bloodthirsty cheers by their supporters; despite the Israeli military bombing homes, hospitals, universities, mosques and churches, intentionally murdering journalists, doctors, babies and the elderly; despite the Israeli military admitting to killing Israeli hostages taken by Hamas, and Israeli Prime Minister Benjamin Netanyahu rejecting Hamas' offer to return all hostages . . . despite all this, the UK has given unconditional support to Israel in what is widely condemned as a genocide – one that has killed 30,000 Palestinians in under four months. It will take many more books to break down the full insanity of this situation, but Western leaders couldn't care less. I can't think of a more damning confirmation that the Western ruling class has not grown out of the racist, cannibalistic impulses that characterised its formation over the past 500 years. The mutilation of

Gaza is framed in Western media as a war, while our social media feeds are filled with the dismembered limbs, desperate cries and nervous breakdowns of Palestinians – not Israelis, as reflected in the death toll. I've never seen anything so evil. The colonisers of the world have united in their support of Israel, to the extent that a map of countries recognising Hamas as a terrorist organisation reads as a map of Western Europe, North America and Australia.

So much of the Western gangsterism I've described in this book is tragically embodied in Israel's latest assault on Gaza. No matter how many times Israeli leaders, political pundits and citizens in general publicly declare their desire to remove Palestinians from the land in order to build new illegal settlements; no matter how openly Israelis mock and celebrate the bombing of Palestinians, while repeating that 'there are no innocents in Gaza', Western leaders continue to insist that Israel is acting in self-defence. Millions of citizens across the global North, many of whom are Jewish, have joined the global South in calling for – at this point, *begging* for – an end to this unbearable slaughter. Through the coverage of such peaceful demonstrations, the role of the media in this colonial world order has become clearer than ever. Mainstream news outlets demonise anything pro-Palestinian as anti-Jewish and pro-'terrorist', whatever that means. Individuals, famous and unknown, have lost employment for supporting Palestine, while the supposedly victimised state of Israel runs expensive propaganda ads at the American Super Bowl. You can't make this up.

In the War on Blackness, music has played a similar role in distorting reality as the news has played throughout this genocide. It has, as Malcolm X warned, attempted to 'make the innocent guilty, and the guilty innocent', by misrepresenting the struggles of the Black working class, heroising violence, selfishness, misogyny and anti-Blackness – the same White supremacist values that terrorised the ancestors of most famous rappers – and projecting a self-destructive, politically disengaged caricature of a demographic that could have applied their talent to organising and educating their communities. Capitalist control of the media has suppressed radical analysis in Black music and mainstream culture in general, initiating young, curious minds into the cult of wealth. Something told me, back in 2015, that the music industry would not be able to reform this behaviour – at least not in time for me to have a viable career. I'm glad I followed my gut and left, but I'm painfully aware that this is not the trend among the majority of Black talent in record deals. Most have been persuaded that there is no life for them outside of what the industry allows, influencing them to accept a fraction of their worth, and completely disregard their potential as voices of change.

However, there's still hope. People will always be people and, as has been proven in the deafening outcry against injustices from Palestine to Congo to Sudan, people hate seeing others suffer. Contrary to the endless stream of Western media portraying human nature as fundamentally selfish, instances of selfless solidarity abound in times like these. I have been inspired by the likes of Marcus 'Redveil' Morton, the nineteen-year-old African American rapper who used his November 2023 appearance at a music festival to broadcast the names of murdered Gazans to an audience of millions while calling for a ceasefire. This, at the start of his career, stands in contrast to Kanye West, one of the wealthiest rappers in the world, who, after ruining his own career with a long string of anti-Black and antisemitic outbursts, insisted he knew nothing about Palestine when questioned, scapegoating his home city of Chicago with the claim that he was more bothered by youth violence back home, which he has done almost nothing about. I find hope in the rise of African music, which broadcasts a joyful, harmonious image of Black life to the world, disproving the longstanding myth that audiences have an in-built preference for violence and misogyny from Black artists. Although I remain concerned about the ability of this music to move beyond non-critical, good-time anthems, I'm still capable of losing myself in its euphoria, and appreciating the smiling, natural Black faces in the music videos of this moment. Hopefully the growing presence of Western capital in Nigeria's music scene especially doesn't lead to the same self-sabotaging messaging we saw in Hip Hop, R&B, Dancehall and other genres of the Black diaspora . . . but we'll see.

It's important to end on this hopeful note. *Track Record* was written at a time of awakening in my life; once I looked past my own journey, my beautiful wife and our precious family, I was jolted out of the urge to over-congratulate myself and redirected towards the global struggle for justice. In this sense, my life is the example I hope to lead with. If I, as a pampered celebrity with a real 'humble beginnings' story, which has led to opportunities spanning different sectors and an audience that reaches across the world – if *I* can turn away from the path of least resistance, and risk losing income and becoming a target of the powerful media interests I've criticised in this book, and open myself up to the smear campaigns that I'm now anticipating for the first time in my career, as a result of things I didn't think I'd ever say aloud, let alone publish in print . . . then you can take on a little risk, too. Our fear of being kicked out of the privileged club is an underrated factor in the perpetuation of suffering. I'm no one's saviour, and I haven't done much other than speak my mind, but I am prepared to follow the truth wherever it may take me. And the truth is, a huge amount of pain in our world is an intentional product of a system that lies about what it really is. This system is held together by people who lie about what they really want. Time and time again, the motivations of these people turn out to be disappointingly basic: they want to remain as close as possible to power. They don't care what this obsession turns them into, or how many of their own they have to sacrifice in order to enjoy their eight decades or so on this planet. A psychotic inability to feel for other humans keeps them driving us all closer to the brink of destruction, and they can't afford for too many of us to pay attention. For this reason, music will always be a heavily controlled arena of ideas. Black music has proven especially useful because, for whatever reason, it's extremely popular, and comes from the bodies of colonised people who can be misdirected, bribed and exploited without enough people noticing, or caring.

Please, my reader, *please* don't look away. Don't try to rationalise the suffering of others, and don't accept different sets of rules for different people – this is the fast track to racism, fascism and generally being a pathetic human being. Use my words to fight for the liberation of everyone everywhere – including our oppressors. I promise to continue expanding the role of art in the struggle for justice, and I promise to tell you the truth when I'm sure of it, study when I'm not, and apologise when I'm wrong. That's the track record I hope to leave behind.

Endnotes

1. Reni Eddo-Lodge, *Why I'm No Longer Talking to White People About Race*, Bloomsbury, 2017
2. Cedric J. Robinson, *Black Marxism: The Making of the Black Radical Tradition*, Penguin Classics, 2021, first published 1983
3. Kehinde Andrews, *Back to Black: Black Radicalism for the 21st Century*, Zed Books, 2018
4. DJ Target, *Grime Kids: The Inside Story of the Global Grime Takeover*, Orion Publishing, 2018
5. Wiley, *Eskiboy*, William Heinemann, 2017
6. Ghetts, 'State of Mind' (ft Andrea Clarke), 2007
   Songwriter: Ghetts
   Label: F**k Radio, The Movement UK & J. Clarke Enterprises
7. Run DMC, 'It's Tricky', 1987
   Songwriters: Joseph Simmonds, Darryl McDaniels, Doug Fieger, Berton Averre
   Label: Profile Records
8. Eric B. & Rakim, 'I Ain't No Joke', 1987
   Songwriters: Eric Barrier, Rakim Allah
   Label: 4th & B'way, Island
9. Kimberlé Crenshaw, 'Demarginalizing the Intersection of Race and Sex', *University of Chicago Legal Forum*, 1989
10. Friedrich Hayek, *The Road to Serfdom*, Routledge Press, 1944

11. Albert Sauvy, 'Trois mondes, une planète', *L'Observateur*, 1952
12. Jeet Heer, 'How the CIA Learned to Rock', *The Nation*, 29 May 2020
13. John L. Potash, *Drugs as Weapons Against Us*, TrineDay, 2014
14. John L. Potash, *The FBI War on Tupac Shakur*, Microcosm Publishing 2021
15. www.youtube.com/watch?v=1-cMd50Ha0E
16. Curtis '50 Cent' Jackson, *Hustle Harder, Hustle Smarter*, Amistad, 2020
17. Renaldo C. McKenzie, *Neoliberalism, Globalization, Income Inequality, Poverty and Resistance*, The Neoliberal Corporation, 2021
18. www.politicshome.com/news/article/home-secretary-suella-braverman-safe-legal-route-migrant-uk; www.bbc.co.uk/news/uk-politics-64282961
19. Howard W. French, *Born in Blackness: Africa, Africans, and the Making of the Modern World, 1471 to the Second World War*, Liveright Publishing Corporation, 2021
20. Harsha Walia, *Border & Rule: Global Migration, Capitalism, and the Rise of Racist Nationalism*, Haymarket Books, 2021
21. C. L. R. James, *The Black Jacobins: Toussaint L'Ouverture and the San Domingo Revolution*, Penguin Classics, 2022, originally published 1938
22. Marlene Daut, 'When France extorted Haiti – the greatest heist in history', theconversation.com, 30 June 2020
23. French, op. cit.
24. www.youtube.com/watch?v=gn9L9RHB8IA
25. Adom Getachew, *Worldmaking After Empire: The Rise and Fall of Self-Determination*, Princeton University Press, 2019

26. Radhika Desai, *Geopolitical Economy: After US Hegemony, Globalization and Empire*, Pluto Press, 2013
27. www.theguardian.com/world/2015/sep/29/how-do-we-know-david-cameron-has-slave-owning-ancestor
28. Walter Rodney, *How Europe Underdeveloped Africa*, Verso, 2018, originally published 1972
29. Eric Williams, *Capitalism and Slavery*, Penguin Modern Classics, 2022, first published 1944; James, op. cit.
30. Kwame Nkrumah, *Neo-Colonialism: The Last Stages of Imperialism*, Thomas Nelson & Sons, 1965; Mehrsa Baradaran, *The Color of Money: Black Banks and the Racial Wealth Gap*, Harvard University Press, 2017